GOD,
I'VE GOT A
QUESTION

# GOD, I'VE GOT A QUESTION

## James Merritt

HARVEST HOUSE PUBLISHERS

EUGENE, OREGON

Published in association with the literary agency of Wolgemuth & Associates.

This book contains stories in which the author has changed people's names and some details of their situations in order to protect their privacy.

*Cover design by Koechel Peterson & Associates, Inc., Minneapolis, Minnesota*

**GOD, I'VE GOT A QUESTION**
Copyright © 2011 by James Merritt
Published by Harvest House Publishers
Eugene, Oregon 97402
www.harvesthousepublishers.com

Library of Congress Cataloging-in-Publication Data
   Merritt, James Gregory, 1952-
   God, I've got a question / James Merritt.
     p. cm.
   Includes bibliographical references (p. ).
   ISBN 978-0-7369-4001-6 (pbk.)
   ISBN 978-0-7369-4002-3 (eBook)
   1. Apologetics. 2. Southern Baptist Convention—Doctrines. I. Title.
   BT1103.M47 2011
   239'.7—dc22

                                   2011007480

11 12 13 14 15 16 17 18 19 / VP-NI / 10 9 8 7 6 5 4 3 2 1

*To my precious mother "Mim"*
*Who from childhood taught me*
*God can always be trusted*

# CONTENTS

# Acknowledgments

This book is one I have often dreamed of writing but honestly never believed the dream would come true. It wouldn't have except for the following risk takers and dream makers.

First, I want to thank my son Jonathan, who prodded and pushed me to get back into writing after a much too long absence. You are such a superior writer to me, and it is a joy for a father to learn from his son. Words could never express my gratitude for your belief in me. For your patience in reviewing the manuscript, your perseverance in encouraging me throughout this project, and your daily presence in my life, I thank you precious son and best friend.

Then I must thank Robert and Erik Wolgemuth, my wonderful literary agents. You are such a joy to work with, and even though I am a little fish in your big sea of clients, you treat me as if I am the second coming of Hemingway. Thanks for your friendship, professionalism, and encouragement.

Working with Harvest House Publishers and their wonderful people has been the most enjoyable experience of any publisher I have ever worked with. Rod Morris, my editor, is just top-shelf. Bob Hawkins, the president of this wonderful company, has become a dear friend and brother whose personal relationship has become a rare treasure in my life. Thanks, Bob, for helping me brainstorm this title in my keeping room as we watched football together. The "Merritt Marriott" is yours anytime.

I want to thank a pastor who is in heaven now but whose book literally rescued my faith when it was sinking in a storm of doubt when I was a college freshman. W.A. Criswell was a pastor unknown to me until someone gave me his book, *Why I Preach the Bible Is Literally True*. It not only set my faith back on firm footing, but it introduced me to a lifelong love for apologetics that is unabated forty years later. God bless you Dr. C—I will see you in heaven again for sure.

I must always praise God for my wonderful family, whose love I bathe and bask in every day: my precious wife of thirty-five years, Teresa; my two other sons/best friends, James and Joshua; my daughter-in-love, Natalie; and my grandson, Harper—Pop's buddy. I love you all more than life itself.

Finally, I pray this book will be used by God to turn doubters into believers and believers into defenders of the faith once for all delivered to the saints. I pray that you who read this book will be moved "in your hearts [to] regard Christ the Lord as holy, always being prepared to make a defense to anyone who asks you for a reason for the hope that is in you" (1 Peter 3:15 ESV).

# The Questions that Claw at Us

*Behold, God is great, and we know him not;*
*the number of his years is unsearchable.*

JOB 36:26 (ESV)

I'll never forget the first time I questioned God. Even now as I reminisce about that event, I can still feel the horror of how a few syllables can rock a faith that had been almost a decade in the making.

It was the fall of 1970. I was a college freshman at Stetson University near Orlando with a seemingly terminal case of homesickness. I remember leaving home thinking that Stetson would be something like Sunday school—it was, after all, Baptist. How I got to a university I had never heard of before the end of my senior year in high school is another story, but suffice to say what I experienced my first few months was a bucket of cold water in my seventeen-year-old face.

I still remember leaving home from Oakwood, a sleepy rural town in Northeast Georgia where my father was raised. Oakwood would make Mayberry look like Beijing. In fact, you could say I lived a Mayberry-esque life. We had one sheriff, no deputy, and a town drunk named Frog whose brother Rabbit was the town barber. Their brother Arthur once ran for mayor on a single promise—"Free water for everybody." (I am not making this up.) At the time of my raising, the total population was 216,[1] and everyone was somehow kin to everyone else either by blood, marriage, or both. Welcome to the Deep South.

No one locked their doors in Oakwood. No one needed to. Everybody planted a garden, the men hunted and fished, the women sewed quilts and canned vegetables, and kids rode bikes and swam in waterholes.

Everyone went to one of the only two churches in town: Oakwood Baptist or Oakwood Methodist. (I honestly didn't know what a Presbyterian, Lutheran, or Catholic was until I went off to college.) I trusted Christ as my Savior and Lord at the age of nine sitting in the local movie theater watching *King of Kings*, and from that moment, my spiritual journey was off to the races.

By the time I was twelve, I thought God spoke King James English, atheists lived only in Communist Russia, and heaven was going to be just one long, homemade-ice-cream social. I skated through childhood without a solitary speed bump in my spiritual journey, never questioning God in any way.

Then I met Professor Lofton.

## A Pin to My Balloon

I arrived on campus and rushed off to sign up for my first college courses. Philosophy sounded like an easy A, so I added it to the list. I would quickly learn that the only thing that would come easy in that class was my confusion.

The first several weeks in Professor Lofton's class passed without incident. We covered seemingly innocuous facts about philosophy and its history. Dr. Lofton seemed nice enough, though definitely on the weird side—he loved to eat bugs he brought to class to illustrate how we allow others to impose arbitrary standards of right and wrong on us. "Bugs aren't so bad," he would say as he crunched down on a ladybug or a caterpillar.

Then one day he brazenly stated in a matter-of-fact voice that he did not believe in the existence of God. He said the only thing that existed was matter and only the visible, material, and temporal constituted reality. Nothing existed that did not have a beginning—and that included the "myth" we know as "God."

My eyes widened like a waist after Thanksgiving dinner. My ears became instant antennae. My heart was racing like Jeff Gordon on the backstretch at the Daytona 500. *You don't believe in God? Everybody believes in God. How can you not believe in God?*

I then boldly and foolishly decided he simply needed a Martin Luther from Oakwood, Georgia, to nail ninety-five theses on "why God *does* exist" to his arrogant philosophical hide.

"Oh yeah," I shouted back with a gotcha smile. "So where did God come from then?"

I thought I'd hit him with my Sunday punch, slinging a question his way that would leave him gasping for philosophical air. Even now, some forty years later, I can still see the wry grin breaking through his scraggly beard.

"From His mother," he said.

All the evangelistic wind was knocked out of me. My head spun and my mind reeled as I tried to gather my spiritual senses. I tried to hide the blow, but I was like a boxer with a swollen eye. Mercifully he stopped the fight himself and invited me to come back whenever I needed another lesson on how to make a fool of myself in front of an atheistic professor of philosophy. But I didn't need to return. The damage had been done.

I trudged back to my dorm not even sure for the first time in my life if God existed. It was the worst feeling I have ever experienced—ever. I tried to pray, but it seemed as if my prayers bounced off the ceiling. I walked outside hoping that with a clear sky and no roof my prayer would make it, but that didn't help. I asked God to forgive me for doubting Him, but all the while I doubted that there was even a God listening.

I called my mom, who was far more spiritual than my dad, but she was no match for the professional skeptic. She encouraged me to call my pastor and alerted him to my situation. When I reached him at home, I was so worried I might drag him down this spiritual drain with me that I was hesitant even to speak. He assured me it was safe to ask him anything, so I unloaded it as if it were burning my hands.

"Where did God come from?" I asked.

I expected a long silence followed by some serious stammering and stuttering. Instead, I received a calm, assured reply: "He didn't come from anywhere. He has neither a beginning nor an ending." He told me about God's eternality and transcendence and shared truths that buoyed my heart.

"But everything on earth had a beginning," I said.

"Yes, but that's because God created everything," he replied. "God is not just another created being. He is the Creator of all created things."

"I don't totally understand all this, and how can I believe in a God I don't understand?"

He then lovingly responded with words that to this day bring unbelievable joy to my heart: "Son, if you could understand everything about God, He wouldn't be God. In fact, He wouldn't be much of a

God to believe in, would He? Just because you can't answer every question doesn't mean God doesn't exist or the question can't be answered by God Himself."

To you, that might seem a "well, duh" moment, but to a homesick freshman from Oakwood it was lifesaving. It was as if I had been in an emotional and spiritual deep freeze, but the warm water of truth had brought feeling back to my extremities. As I hung up the phone, I felt confident that I could face life's pressing questions without fear.

## Of Course We Question

You may not be questioning the existence of God, but I bet you have a spiritual inquiry nagging you from time to time. Don't fret. We know God personally but not perfectly, truly but not totally, experientially but not exhaustively. It is natural that finite creatures like us would have questions about an infinite Creator like God.

Here is the good news: God is neither surprised nor offended by our questions. In fact, the Bible is full of questions—3,294 to be exact. God wants us to bring our questions to Him and give Him a shot at providing an answer.

As a pastor of five churches over thirty-five years, I have fielded hundreds of questions from skeptics, seekers, sinners, and saints. Many of those questions pop up again and again. As it turns out, certain questions claw at us all.

I wish I could say that I always had answers, but I can't. Too often early in my ministry my answers ranged from the glib to the thoughtless. As a young minister, I was reluctant to admit "I'm not sure," or worse, "I don't know." I thought that a pastor should *always* have an answer even if I didn't.

Now I'm ready to admit that no one can answer every inquiry about the God who bluntly tells us,

"For my thoughts are not your thoughts,
    neither are your ways my ways," declares the LORD.
"As the heavens are higher than the earth,
    so are my ways higher than your ways
    and my thoughts than your thoughts."

Isaiah 55:8-9

Yet, for the most frequent questions I have been asked, I have found certain answers that bring peace and satisfaction to questioning minds and breaking hearts. These answers are, like buried treasure, to be discovered and mined from the only One who can give us those answers. In fact, you will see that much of God's Word was written in anticipation of the questions we all find ourselves asking.

In the pages that follow, we will wrestle together with some of the most frequently asked questions about God, faith, life, and the world around us. You will hear true stories of people I've encountered who sought an answer that will bring spiritual peace and intellectual satisfaction.

I make no promises that every answer will cure every doubt in your mind. At times, I must simply say, "I don't know." On other occasions, we must remember that faith and not reason alone is the only antidote to doubt. As Blaise Pascal, the seventeenth-century French philosopher and theologian, stated, "There is sufficient light for those who desire to see, and there is sufficient darkness for those of a contrary disposition."[2]

I am convinced that the God who knows every heart and every thought has yet to meet a question that stumps Him. So I make only one promise: As we explore these questions together, we will discover answers from the Bible that will both comfort the heart and challenge the mind to go deeper with God than ever before. If that happens to both you and me, then every honest question will have been well worth the asking.

# God, Is the Bible
# Really Your Word?

I am not sure how Bart found our church, but I'm glad he did. Bart is a skeptic by nature and had wandered into our church with a pocketful of questions about God, Christianity, faith, Jesus, and the church. I love apologetics, and I would rather witness to the "convert me if you can, buddy" type than the "I am so ready to become a Christian, where do I sign?" type. (You can occasionally find the latter, though more rarely as our culture becomes more secular.) Bart was just what I wanted.

When I was informed of his interest, I set up an appointment to go to his house hoping to build a bridge to his heart. He intrigued me from the beginning. Bart reminded me of the rich young ruler, except he was anything but rich. A graduate of The Citadel, his military background and training was evident from his firm handshake, confident demeanor, and his look-you-in-the-eye attentiveness. He was flanked by his family—a sweet wife who longed for Bart to come to faith and beautiful children. As I found out more about his background, I was warmly drawn to the military code of honor ingrained in his DNA.

No small talk for Bart. He got right to the point as he began firing questions at me as if I were the target and his tongue were an AK-47. "Why are you a Christian? What is it about Jesus that is so different? How can I ever believe?" It became obvious quickly that the "God loves you and has a wonderful plan for your life" approach would get about as far as Rush Limbaugh at an ACLU convention.

That night has now turned into a two-year conversation built around breakfasts, lunches, office meetings, and discussions about books I have given him by authors ranging from Lee Strobel to Josh McDowell. Frankly, it has been both frustrating and exhilarating. Sometimes it has been "three steps forward and two steps back"; at other times it has been "two steps back, forget forward."

The most enlightening meeting we had was our third one at a Cracker Barrel not far from our church. (I am convinced that the one place you can always feel the presence of the Holy Spirit, besides the church, is a Cracker Barrel.) I had moved Bart from atheism to agnosticism fairly early by admitting that no one can either prove or disprove the existence of God. He readily grasped the fact that taking an "I don't know whether God exists or not" position is far more defensible than claiming an "I know for sure there is no God" approach that is possible only with perfect omniscience. Allowing for the possibility of a God enabled us to make progress on the spiritual track we were on together.

As we waited on our breakfasts, we began the same procedure of circling each other like two boxers in the first round of a major title fight—neither wanted the other to land the first blow, and both wanted to avoid the dreaded knockdown.

"Bart," I began, "contrary to most philosophers, the most important question about God is not 'Is there a God?'" That is what the infamous Dr. Lofton said that day in class and what most people assume is *the* question about any supreme being.

"It's not," Bart said with eyes wide and eyebrows arched.

"No." I allowed a pause to get heavily pregnant before I continued. "The most important question about God is this: 'If there is a God, has that God spoken?'[1] Bart, let's assume that there is a God. Let's retire for the time being any atheistic or agnostic thoughts. I know that's a big jump for you, but humor me for a moment."

Bart shifted uncomfortably in his seat and reluctantly agreed to my scenario. I then took my AK-47 and began my rapid-fire salvo.

"Does this God have a name? Does He know me? Does He care for me? Does He have a plan for my life? Can I have a relationship with Him? If so, how? What does He consider right and wrong? Is there life after death? Can I have a relationship with Him that transcends time and space? How can I live in such a way that pleases Him and keeps me on His good side? Why did He put me here?"

As our breakfast was served, the look on his face was that of a boxer saved by the bell. I could tell he was trying to get his intellectual equilibrium back to counter what I admit was a self-conscious effort to knock him off balance and take the offensive early.

He picked at his food, obviously deep in thought, then looked at me and admitted, "I don't know how I could come up with the answers to those questions."

I put my hand on his shoulder and said, "Bart, *you can't* come up with those answers on your own, and neither could a thousand Einsteins. The only way we can know the answers to those questions is if God Himself told us—what's known as divine revelation."

"So you obviously believe that God has spoken through the Bible."

"Yes."

Bart then leaned back in his chair and said, "That is a big problem because I don't believe the Bible is God's Word any more than I believe that this morning's newspaper is. Both were written by men who we both know can and do make mistakes. Besides, at least today's newspaper can be verified by present-day witnesses and other corroborating evidence. Why should I believe a book that is two thousand years old? After all, you are basing *everything you believe* on the Bible aren't you?"

I looked at Bart and thought that Jesus must have had similar feelings as He looked at the rich young ruler. On the one hand, I believed that Bart was being sincere in his question; on the other hand, I was saddened by his striking admission of complete skepticism toward God's Word.

(I give Bart a lot of credit for asking a legitimate question. It's a question not only to be expected from an unbeliever but seriously contemplated by every believer as well. If you are a believer, let me ask you, "Why *do you* believe the Bible?" I suspect that most believers have not thought through this question, and if faced with a Bart, would quickly feel cotton in their mouths. It's one thing to know what you believe; it's another thing altogether to know *why* you believe it.)

I took a deep breath and affirmed the legitimacy of Bart's question. "Bart, you have raised a great question that reveals more about the differences we have than you think. I appreciate you giving me the opportunity to answer a question that will take us even farther down the road than I had hoped for at this meeting. Do you have the time for a very thorough answer?"

He laughed. "I only have an hour."

"Then you just committed to another meeting, because an hour won't be enough time."

"Seriously?" he said.

I was deadly serious, and you'll see why as I unfold to you my response to Bart over our next two meetings. I began by explaining the concept of a worldview, which is foundational to dealing with any essential question.

First, *everybody has a worldview*. Everybody has a set of assumptions and presuppositions that determine the way they look at the world, their place in the world, and what they think in the world is really important. Regardless of your creed, religion, faith, or lack thereof, you bring to the table certain preconceived beliefs and codes that affect your view of truth, morality, and life itself.

---

> Everybody looks at this world through certain assumptions and presuppositions, some provable, some nonprovable. The Christian cannot prove that God exists, but the atheist cannot prove that God doesn't. Both worldviews are based on faith.

---

Second, *there are only two basic worldviews—the Christian worldview and the non-Christian worldview*. These worldviews are radically different at practically every point. Whether it is answering questions such as:

- Why is there something rather than nothing?
- How do you explain human nature?
- How do you determine what is right and wrong?
- How do you know that you know?
- What happens to a person at death?

the Christian worldview gives answers radically different from every other non-Christian worldview.

Third, *every worldview is based on faith*. Everybody looks at this world through certain assumptions and presuppositions, some provable, some nonprovable. The Christian has a worldview based on the belief that God exists. The atheist has a worldview based on the belief that God doesn't. The Christian cannot prove that God exists, but the atheist cannot prove that God doesn't. Both worldviews are based on faith. The question is, which worldview has the strongest evidence to support the faith of its adherents?

Fourth, *every worldview is only as valid as the evidence it is based upon.* When answering essential questions, this concept must be kept in mind. It is at this point that the so-called "culture wars" are being waged. Chuck Colson put it this way: "The culture war is not just about abortion, homosexual rights, or the decline of public education. These are only skirmishes. The real war is a cosmic struggle between worldviews—between the Christian worldview and the various secular and spiritual worldviews arrayed against it."[2]

The first Sunday I was away at college, I attended a church and went to the small group (it was called Sunday school back then) for college students. As soon as the class started, a man got up without saying a word and wrote three questions on a chalkboard:

- Who am I?
- Why am I here?
- Where am I going?

Mr. West would repeat that task every Sunday and then challenge us with some thought-provoking comments. After the first couple of Sundays, he arrested my attention with this declaration: "One word will determine what we believe and why we believe it. That word is *truth.*"

Which worldview is true? Better, which worldview gives the right answers to those questions? If we are unable to answer those questions correctly, we have no discernible purpose or meaning to life.

The Christian worldview goes beyond all other worldviews in one crucially important respect: It asserts not just truth but *ultimate eternal* truth. The Christian worldview provides answers for the three key themes that alone tell us what is wrong with the world and how it can be made right again, namely, creation, fall, and redemption.

The doctrine of creation tells us we are not evolutionary accidents. We are a direct creation of the Creator of the universe. Practically all other worldviews deny this concept.

At the same time, it is obvious something is wrong with this God-created world; either God blew it or this is not exactly the world God created. The Christian worldview tells us the problem is the introduction of sin into the world by the fall of mankind in the Garden of Eden. Sin has corrupted the entire human race as well as the physical world we live in. The non-Christian view invariably denies that sin has anything to do with our problem.

Finally, the Christian worldview tells us redemption is the only solution to the problem. We need a Savior to remedy the sin problem and to give mankind a new heart and a new mind that is truly centered on God. The non-Christian worldview denies the need for personal redemption at all.

> To many non-Christians, the Bible is no more than an antiquated collection of myths and fables. To others it is a good book, but it is not *God's* book.

If you are a believer reading this, then I know I am singing to the choir. But if you are a Bart, or even a nominal Christian, your question still remains, "But you get this view from only one source—the Bible—so why believe the Bible as opposed to any other truth source, religious writing, or human reasoning?"

I concede it is not only a fair question but an inflammatory one given today's culture.

Most of this world denies that it is important to believe the Bible or even to consider it anything other than just another book. Recently, the Colorado Supreme Court threw out the sentence of a man given the death penalty because jurors consulted the Bible in reaching a verdict. The court said this constituted an improper outside influence and a reliance on a "higher authority."[3] The Supreme Court of Colorado was saying in essence it is improper to consult the Bible because it is just another book.

To many non-Christians, the Bible is no more than an antiquated collection of myths and fables. To others it is a good book, but it is not *God's* book. On the other hand, two billion people, roughly one-third of this world's population, claim to believe in the God of this book and to believe this is the book God wrote. Even the men who wrote it believed they were writing the very words of God.

---

Jesus Christ made the ultimate statement
concerning any word inspired by God's Spirit when
He said to the Father: "Your word is truth."

---

The biggest challenge to unbelievers—and their biggest objection to the Bible—is that *it claims to be not just the words of men, but the Word of God*. In the Old Testament alone, phrases such as, "God said" or "God spoke" or "the Word of the Lord came" occur nearly four thousand times (seven hundred times in the first five books, forty times in one chapter). Hundreds of years later, the apostle Paul said this about the Bible: "All Scripture is inspired by God and is useful to teach us what is true and to make us realize what is wrong in our lives. It corrects us when we are wrong and teaches us to do what is right" (2 Timothy 3:16 NLT).

Yet Jesus Christ made the ultimate statement concerning any word inspired by God's Spirit when He said to the Father: "Your word is truth."[4]

Now don't miss the tremendous amount of ground Jesus covered with this statement. Jesus was not just stating that the Bible speaks truth. He was stating that this book is the very essence of truth and the standard by which all other "truth" is to be measured. Furthermore, this statement was made in a prayer Jesus was offering to God the Father. He was calling this word God's Word. This book is God's Word because it is truth and it is truth because it is God's Word. But if this statement is true, there should be compelling reasons to believe the Bible is not just reliable truth but divine truth.

> My father taught me that "a man is no better than his word." Well, neither is God, and He is perfectly willing to lay His reputation on the line behind the veracity of His Word.

Put another way, a book truly written by God Himself should bear certain verifying marks and evidence that would confirm a divine imprint on its contents. Why? Because God will be judged by His words just as we are by ours. Think of how my skills as a writer, thinker, and researcher will be judged by those who read this book. Beginning with my editor, then my proofreaders, then my publisher, and finally my readers, this book will always be a reflection of me. How much more is God's Word a reflection of His character, nature, and reliability? Perhaps that is why we read in the book of Psalms:

> for you have exalted above all things
> your name and your word.[5]

My father taught me early in life "a man is no better than his word." Well, neither is God, and He is perfectly willing to lay His reputation on the line behind the veracity of His Word. But we should have solid reasons for believing that the Bible is God's very word(s), and here are four reasons to support this claim.

## The Bible Is Historically Reliable

What would happen if you chose ten different people from the same city to write a book about one controversial topic, such as the meaning of life? Now add these parameters: they share the same culture, same educational level, and the same language, but they are separated from each other, never allowed to talk to or consult each other. What are the chances that what they wrote would be in total agreement? You and I both know the chance of that happening would be zero.

Now imagine a book that is actually sixty-six books in one, written over a period of fifteen hundred years by forty different authors living on three different continents (Europe, Africa, and Asia), writing in three different languages (Hebrew, Greek, and Aramaic) on many controversial topics, and yet all concentrating on one basic theme and all being in perfect agreement on their theological conclusions.

> Nobody can prove or disprove what has
> taken place in the past. All one can
> do is present the evidence.

Would you expect there to be a literary symmetry from beginning to end with the last book being written well over a thousand years after the first one? Consider this: Genesis, the first book of the Bible, begins in a garden in paradise. In the middle of that garden are the tree of life and the tree of the knowledge of good and evil.[6] When you go to the last book of the Bible, Revelation, written some fifteen hundred years later, you end up again in the paradise of God and there once again is the tree of life "for the healing of the nations."[7] In Genesis, man is driven out of the garden because of his sin and to keep him from eating of the tree that would have sealed his physical and spiritual death.[8] In Revelation, he is invited to partake of the tree that symbolizes his eternal life and the removal of the curse. In Genesis, a river flows from the garden. In Revelation, a river flows from the throne of God. The golden thread that runs from Genesis to Revelation is the theme of redemption through blood sacrifice: lambs in the Old Testament and the lamb of God in the New Testament.[9]

But how do we know that all that the Bible says actually happened? How do we know it is fact not fable? How do we really know there was a Moses and a Red Sea crossing? How do we know there was a Goliath that David killed? How do we know there was a Daniel in the lion's den? How do we know there was a Jesus, who died on a cross and came out of a tomb three days later? What reasons do we have to believe the Bible?

Admittedly, nobody can prove or disprove what has taken place in the past. All one can do is present the evidence. I can't prove there actually was a man named George Washington who served as the first president of the United States. All I can do is present the evidence. Here we need to keep two things in mind:

1. The trustworthiness of any ancient historical account is based on the evidence for that account.

2. The evidence must come from ancient documents and manuscripts. All ancient history is based on documentary evidence. Remember, DVDs, videos, televisions, and tape recorders didn't exist a hundred years ago.

Furthermore, critics love to point out that we don't have access to any of the original documents penned by the biblical authors. We don't have the original manuscripts that were first written when all these things took place. So how do we know we have the right stuff? How do we know Jesus even existed? How do we know we are reading actual historical events not made up myths? We are relying on accounts two to three millennia old. Well, to these critics we can enthusiastically say, "Glad you asked!"

Have you ever heard of Julius Caesar? Ever read the writings of Plato? Studied Homer's *Iliad*? Have you ever heard of anyone questioning the existence of any of those historical figures? Any professor of literature ever declare that Caesar was no more real than Mickey Mouse or that the *Iliad* really wasn't written by Homer? Not lately…probably not ever.

---

The number of manuscripts we have supporting the New Testament alone is almost forty times the number of manuscripts supporting the writings of Julius Caesar, Plato, and Homer combined.

---

Yet these assumed to be actual historical figures and literary works have relatively shaky authentication compared to the Bible. Have you ever thought about how many copies or manuscripts we have of the ancient writings of these men and how close in time those documents are to their subject? Have you ever thought about what the time span is between the copies that we do have and the original documents? Let me just give you the manuscript evidence for the ancient writings for these three historical figures.

*Julius Caesar*—earliest manuscripts one thousand years after Caesar lived; only ten manuscripts exist.

*Plato*—earliest manuscripts thirteen hundred years after Plato lived; only 7 manuscripts exist.

*Homer*—earliest manuscripts five hundred years after Homer lived; 643 manuscripts exist. Homer's *Iliad* has the

best manuscript support of any ancient text in the world
next to the Bible.

Now consider this—there are over 24,000 partial and full Greek
manuscripts of the New Testament, the earliest one dating from just
thirty five years after the book of Revelation was written. The number of manuscripts we have supporting the New Testament alone is
almost forty times the number of manuscripts supporting the writings of the aforementioned historical figures combined. And the earliest manuscripts are just one generation removed from the oldest New
Testament book.

What about the Old Testament (which as you could guess is much
older than the New Testament)? Recently I was in Qumran at the site
of the discovery of the Dead Sea Scrolls. Fragments of almost every
book in the Old Testament were found in these scrolls dated approximately 150 BC, only two hundred years after the last event of the Old
Testament took place.

*No other book from the ancient world has as much manuscript support
or is as closely tied to the original event as the Bible.*

Putting together all of these manuscripts and comparing them with
the version of the Bible we have today, we now know that we have at
least 99.5 percent of what would be considered the original document.
No other ancient historical source can make that claim. But Bart still
needed to ask, "How do we know they got their history right?" It is
one thing to accurately record something, but that does not prove the
veracity of the thing recorded.

If I read a history book that says Custer's Last Stand took place at
Yankee Stadium while he was eating a chili dog in 1998, I would be
disinclined to believe that history book. The number of manuscripts
verifying the accuracy of the transmission of that account would be

irrelevant. However, we have a tool to verify the historical accuracy of a document, and that tool is archaeology.

There are hundreds of examples of how archaeology has confirmed the Bible, and entire books have been written on this one subject. I will give you just one. You probably have heard the story of how Joshua "fought the battle of Jericho and the walls came tumbling down." For many years liberal critics denigrated this story as completely fabricated for several reasons. First, walls don't just fall down flat because someone walks around them. Second, the Israelites could not have marched around that city seven times in one day because the city was too large. In many academic circles, the light of this story had been eclipsed by the facts on the ground.

---

*It is illogical to think that the God who created a universe that operates according to the scientific principles He built into it would not communicate in a scientifically accurate way.*

---

Then Professor John Garstang, a British archaeologist, excavated the site of ancient Jericho and discovered that the walls of the city had fallen so completely that the attackers were able to climb up and over the ruins into the city. Why was that so unusual? Because the evidence showed the walls had collapsed outward. Walls do not fall outward; when they are attacked, they fall inward. But in this case just the opposite occurred—just as the book of Joshua records.

I recently visited this ancient site for the seventeenth time. Jericho is actually smaller than the seventy acres my church sits on. I could walk around Jericho seven times in one morning and then go play golf before lunch. It was entirely possible for the people of Israel to march around this city much more than seven times in one day.

This one illustration is just the tip of the iceberg of the incredible archaeological confirmation of the Bible's veracity. Dr. Nelson Glueck, by consensus the greatest modern authority on Israeli archaeology, said, "No archeological discovery has ever controverted a biblical reference… archeology continues to confirm a clear outline or in exact detail historical statements in the Bible."[10]

As Jesus said, "Your word is truth."[11]

## The Bible Is Scientifically Correct

The Bible is not a science book, but if it is true and if it is God's Word, then just as you expect it to be historically reliable, you would expect it to be scientifically accurate. It is illogical to think that the God who created a universe that operates according to the scientific principles He built into it would not communicate in a scientifically accurate way. Another striking evidence that this book is divine truth and God's Word is that many of the principles of modern science were recorded as facts of nature in the Bible long before any scientist ever confirmed them.

Years ago many believed that the world was flat. Columbus had to overcome this popular opinion in order to finance the voyage that led to his discovery of America. Columbus was convinced as he sailed from Spain that he not only would not "sail over the edge" but that he would eventually find his way back to Spain. He wrote in his diary: "For the execution of the voyage to the Indies, I did not make use of intelligence, mathematics or maps. It is simply the fulfillment of what Isaiah had prophesied."[12] What prophecy from Isaiah was Columbus referring to?

> He sits enthroned above the circle of the earth,
>     and its people are like grasshoppers.
> He stretches out the heavens like a canopy,
>     and spreads them out like a tent to live in.[13]

Columbus was convinced that the world was a circle,[14] not flat, and that there was no danger at all of "sailing off the sea." It never occurred to him that Scripture would be scientifically unreliable.

---

Thirty percent of the Bible consists of prophecy,
and not one of its prophecies has ever
been shown to be false.

---

Take the science of meteorology. You would expect the Master Meteorologist to know far more than your television weatherman. Years ago scientists thought that winds blew always in a straight direction. Of course, meteorologists now know that wind travels within circuits called "jet streams." God's Word spoke of them before Christ was born:

> Blowing toward the south,
> Then turning toward the north,
> The wind continues swirling along;
> And on its circular courses the wind returns.[15]

Until fairly recent times, doctors saw no need for washing their hands. Many people died from the hands of doctors themselves because they carried on those hands the very germs that would infect and kill their patients. Later, doctors began to wash their hands in still water, but the mortality rate remained high from infection caught from the very doctor who was trying to bring healing. Today, any doctor will tell you always to wash hands in running water to make sure the germs are washed away. Where did that lifesaving medical idea come from? "Now when the man with the discharge becomes cleansed from his discharge, then he shall count off for himself seven days for his cleansing; he shall then wash his clothes and bathe his body in running water and will become clean."[16]

We now know that our first president, George Washington, died from a combination of pneumonia worsened by severe blood loss. The blood loss came from a common cure for many serious illnesses in the day—attaching leeches to the skin of the patient to "bleed" the illness out of the body. Usually the opposite effect happened: the patient would die from losing blood, the greatest source of energy and infection fighting power his body had. If only doctors had taken this verse seriously from a medical standpoint: "For the life of a creature is in the blood."[17]

As Jesus said "Your word is truth."

## The Bible Is Prophetically Accurate

I would be hard-pressed to deny the veracity of the Bible just because of its incredible prophetic content and accuracy. No other book on this planet can match the Bible's staggering accuracy in foretelling events. Thirty percent of the Bible consists of prophecy, and not one of its prophecies has ever been shown to be false.

Many of the prophecies of Scripture are so specific and so detailed they demand an exact fulfillment. Jesus Himself fulfilled at least forty-eight different prophecies concerning everything from His lineage to His birth, death, and resurrection. The odds of any one person doing that would be one in ten to the 157th power.[18]

---

God's truth should go beyond
accuracy; it must be transforming.

---

Not only that, many prophecies predicted extraordinary events, such as a virgin birth. In hundreds of instances, the fulfillment of the prophecy did not take place until after the prophet had already died.

In the Old Testament alone, over two thousand prophecies have already come to pass. Nothing vaguely resembles this in any other book in the world. Twenty-six books claim to be divine Scriptures like the Bible, but not one of those volumes has any specific predictive prophecies.

The Bible even does something unparalleled in any other literary work. It gives detailed predictions concerning entire countries, some of which are being fulfilled in the twenty-first century. One such fascinating example came to my attention.

At one time, Egypt was the greatest nation in the entire world. It was the king of nations. It was the richest country on earth. In one prophecy about Egypt, the prophet Ezekiel said, "There shall no longer be a prince from the land of Egypt."[19]

Until a few decades ago, before Egypt adopted a more democratic form of government, a prince always ruled her. But during the nearly twenty-five hundred years between this prophecy and Egypt's change to its present form of government, none of its princes were Egyptian. That would be like prophesying today that an American will never again be president of the United States and then having twenty-five hundred years go by with no American president.

How could anybody have predicted something like that? Only God could, who knows everything that will happen before it occurs and whose predictions become, by necessity, commands that must be obeyed.

As Jesus said, "Your word is truth."

## The Bible Is Personally Transforming

Even if you have bought what I have been selling in this chapter, I still have one other thing to point out about the world's bestselling book that should motivate believing it above all else. When I say the Bible is true, I mean the Bible is factual—it accurately records historical events. It is scientifically true—one should never worry about established scientific fact contradicting spiritual truth. It is prophetically true—it predicts many events that happened exactly as prophesied.

But God's truth should go beyond accuracy; it must be transforming. Something can be true and factual, but have no personal, spiritual significance. I can tell you the truth about how many buttons I have on the shirt I'm wearing right now, but who gives a rip? When I talk about the Bible being true, I mean it is *transformationally* true—it is capable of bringing about personal, spiritual, and eternal change in one's life.

Years ago I was pastoring a church in Laurel, Mississippi, and I had just finished preaching a sermon on the reality of hell (don't hear many of those any more). Afterward a man came up to me and asked if he could see me in my office. After we sat down, he asked, "Do you *really* believe what you preached today?" I assured him I did. He then asked if I *really* cared whether people went to hell or not, and slightly miffed, I affirmed that I did. He then said, "Good. I want you to promise me you will go talk to my wife." I told him I would be glad to. He made me promise again, to my great irritation, that I would. He then said with a sly gotcha grin, "You need to know two things about Diane—she is an atheist and she hates preachers. But you promised you would go."

I left my office feeling as if I had just been suckered into buying some beachfront property in Phoenix, Arizona. Nevertheless, on the following Tuesday night, Teresa and I made our way out to a double-wide trailer in 95 degree heat with all of the enthusiasm of facing a colonoscopy. (Now that I have had two, that is *exactly* how I felt.) We walked up to the door and were greeted by a lady wearing her hair in a bun, looking at us through thick black glasses with a scowl as menacing as a mother bear whose cubs have just been threatened.

"Who are you and what do you want?" she demanded.

I wanted to say "Avon calling," but instead I introduced us and said,

"I'm the pastor of Highland Church and wanted to know if we could come in and visit with you."

"I'm an atheist and I hate preachers," she spat out with more than a little venom.

"I know," I said. "I've heard so much about you. But seeing as how we drove ten miles out here in this hot weather, could we have ten minutes of your time?"

"I'll give you two."

I decided to forego the usual ice-breaking small talk and jumped in: "Diane, do you know for sure when you die you will go to heaven?"

"I told you I'm an atheist. I don't even believe in heaven—and I know there is no God."

Praying hard and thinking fast, I said, "Diane, I don't believe you are an atheist."

"Why not?"

"Let me ask you a question. Do you know everything there is to know about everything?"

"No, of course not."

"Would you say you know half of everything there is to know about everything?"

"No."

"Well, let's just pretend you do. Would you agree that in that body of knowledge you do not possess, God could exist?"

"Wow! I never thought about that. Well, to be honest, I don't *know* there is no God. I'm just not sure whether there is or not."

"Now we're getting somewhere. You're not an atheist, you're an agnostic."

She smiled triumphantly. "Yes, that's what I am, an agnostic." (I didn't tell her the Latin word for 'agnostic' was 'ignoramus'—I didn't think that would move things along in a positive fashion.)

"Now, are you an honest agnostic or a dishonest agnostic?"

"What do you mean?" she said through a puzzled look.

"Well, an honest agnostic says, 'I don't know whether there is a god or not, but I'm willing to find out.' A dishonest agnostic says, 'I don't know whether there is a god or not, and I don't want to know.' Which one are you?"

"Well…I guess I'm an honest agnostic."

I asked her to wait in her chair. I went out to my car and brought her a New Testament. "This is a Bible. I want you to begin reading the Gospel of John, and I want you to read one chapter a day. After you've read each chapter, I want you to ask yourself two questions: Who did Jesus claim to be, and what am I going to do about it?"

She gasped. "I don't believe one thing in the Bible."

"Then it will do you no harm to read it. John has 21 chapters, so it'll take you three weeks to read it. You won't hear from me for three weeks. After you've finished, with your permission Teresa and I will come back and see where you are in your spiritual pilgrimage."

I then bid her goodbye as Teresa and I got up to leave.

"Wait!" she almost screamed. "I don't believe the Bible."

"I don't care," I said nonchalantly as I got in my car. "See you in three weeks."

This was Tuesday. On Sunday morning after I preached, I gave an altar call for people who wanted to commit themselves to Christ. To my palpable shock, here came Diane down the aisle smiling broadly as she reached out her hand to me. Showing my great faith in the transforming power of the Bible, I clumsily asked, "Why have you come?"

With a smile as bright as a full moon on a clear night, she said," I want to be baptized and join this church."

"Diane, you can't do that until you've trusted Christ as your Lord and Savior."

"I have."

"When?"

"Wednesday morning."

"But…"

She giggled. "I didn't get past the first chapter."

That evening I baptized Diane, and she became one of the most committed and faithful members of our church.

I could tell you of many more like Diane, individuals such as Pravera, who recently came to our church and told me over breakfast how he was converted to Christ from Hinduism by closeting himself with the Bible, reading it from cover to cover, and concluding that Jesus was who He claimed to be. Pravera trusted Christ on his own in his bedroom. This world has billions of people whose lives have been eternally transformed by hearing the Bible preached or reading it on their own and believing. I challenge anyone to show me any religious work ever written that has such transformational power.

Our second president, John Adams, put it best when he wrote in his diary. "Suppose a nation in some distant region should take the Bible for their only law book and every member should regulate his conduct by the precepts there exhibited!…What a utopia, what a paradise would this region be."[20]

In the end, there is one essential question about the Bible: Does it express our ideas about God or God's ideas about us? Is it God's Word to us or our words about God?[21] Everybody on this planet has to make a decision. There are many sacred writings and religious books all saying different things about God, heaven, hell, creation, sin, redemption, and salvation.[22] When it comes to these varying truth claims, there can be only two options. Option 1: they are all wrong. Option 2: only one is right.

Perhaps the Bible could be just a bunch of myths and fairy tales, but the overwhelming evidence suggests otherwise. Some other religious book may be the real truth and the Bible could be totally wrong but again the evidence indicates the Bible can more than stand on its own against all other religious authorities combined.

John Wesley, the founder of the Methodist Church, spoke best when he said, "I am a creature of a day. I am a spirit come from God and returning to God. I want to know one thing: the way to heaven. God Himself has condescended to teach me the way. He has written it down in a book. Give me that book! At any price give me the Book of God. Let me be a man of one book—this book, the Bible."[23]

No, Bart is still not convinced, but it has nothing to do with the evidence. As I said to him recently, "I have decided I am going to go with the man who came back from the dead, who said, 'Your word is truth.' I am going with the Bible."

# CHAPTER TWO

# I Don't Understand...
# How Can You Be
# One God in Three Persons?

The call came from a buddy I had led to Christ many years ago. He had battled with drugs among other things before becoming a Christian, and though he had come a long way, I never expected to hear these words from his mouth: "Pastor, I met a banker recently who wants to have dinner with you. I've been sharing Christ with him and haven't gotten far. He wants to meet with you because you're a pastor."

I was pleasantly surprised to hear that my friend had been sharing Christ with anyone, but my surprise intensified with his next statement: "This man is a devout Muslim and wants to ask you a question."

"Of course, I would be glad to meet with him," I said. "Set it up."

We met at a nice restaurant, and I was introduced to a dignified-looking gentleman with a gentle demeanor and warm smile. I took a liking to him immediately. After ordering our dinner and exchanging pleasantries, I immediately took the plunge.

"Mast, I understand that you have some questions for me. Fire away."

With a demure smile he leaned across the table. "If you can explain the Trinity to me, I would be open to considering Christianity."

(I almost felt like saying, "Let me explain the theory of relativity instead—that would be far easier.")

"Why is that your only question?" I said.

"Because I believe in only one God, and I think you believe in three. I don't see where either Jesus or your Holy Spirit ever claim to be God, so why do you accept the Trinity as truth? I am convinced that the Trinity is the one roadblock that I cannot overcome."

---

If you were to ask God the Father, Jesus Christ, and the Holy Spirit, "Will the real God please stand up?" all three would have to stand in order to tell the truth.

---

As I sat there pondering his question, my mind raced over to another country an ocean away—the Holy Land. I have been to Israel many times, and without question one of the most distinctive and beautiful architectural sites there is the Dome of the Rock. It is the masterpiece of Islamic architecture. It was erected in 691 AD to enshrine the rock where Islamic tradition holds that Abraham sacrificed his son Isaac. If you look carefully, you'll notice the geometry of a dome supported by an octagon-shaped building. It is meant to symbolize the transition from earth to heaven, but the building also is an Islamic symbol stating that Islam is the supreme and only true religion and worships the only true God. Here is one of the Koranic inscriptions that decorates this building:

People of the Book do not transgress the bounds of your reli-
gion. Speak nothing but the truth about Allah. The Messiah,
Jesus, the son of Mary was no more than Allah's apostle and
His Word which he conveyed to Mary: a spirit from him.
So believe in Allah and his apostles and do not say: "Three."
Forbear and it shall be better for you. Allah is but one god.
Allah forbid that he should have a son (*Koran 4:1*)![1]

That inscription is a direct attack and a dogmatic denial of one of
the most important doctrines taught in the entire Bible—the doctrine
of the Trinity. In all fairness, Islam is not alone in opposing this belief—
or the related belief of the Incarnation.

Irrationality has been the yoke put around the neck of the Incarnation and the Trinity. How can Jesus be both fully God and fully man
at one and the same time? How can one God be three persons simul-
taneously? Thomas Jefferson scornfully remarked:

When we shall have done away with the incomprehensible
jargon of the Trinitarian arithmetic, that three are one and
one is three; when we shall have knocked down the artificial
scaffolding, reared to mask from view the very simple structure of Jesus; when, in short, we shall have learned everything which has been taught since his day and got back to
the pure and simple doctrines he inculcated, we shall then
be truly and worthily his disciples.[2]

Yet if the biblical witness is true, if you were to ask God the Father,
Jesus Christ, and the Holy Spirit, "Will the real God please stand up?"
all three would have to stand in order to tell the truth.

In this chapter we are going to explore without question one of the
most difficult doctrines in the entire Bible. I begin with three foundational statements that will serve as guardrails to keep us from getting off
any exit of misunderstanding or misinterpretation. Biblically, accepting

the truth of all three statements is necessary to know God, to properly understand Him, and to enter into a personal relationship with Him:

1. There is one God—eternal and indivisible.
2. This one God is three persons—each distinct from the other.
3. Each person is fully God—coequal, coexistent, and co-eternal.

This is one of the greatest distinctives of Christianity. No other religion in the world is a Trinitarian religion. Judaism, Islam, Jehovah's Witnesses, and Unitarians all deny the doctrine of the Trinity. One objection given is the term is not even found in the Bible. Indeed, the term was not coined until approximately 160 AD by the early church father Tertullian.[3] But this statement, though true, is irrelevant. The concept of the Trinity is found throughout the Bible though the term is not.[4]

---

The simple reason the Trinity is a mystery is that it is about God, and God Himself is a mystery.

---

Paul, in closing his second letter to the Corinthian church, gave a classic Trinitarian benediction that points to a triune God: "May the grace of the Lord Jesus Christ, and the love of God, and the fellowship of the Holy Spirit be with you all."[5] Paul's appeal on behalf of the believers in Corinth is to a Triune God, for only God is omnipresent, and these divine persons are present with all believers. Like Paul, I say unapologetically, if you are going to know God, you must know God as Trinity or you cannot know God at all.

## God's Majesty Is Also a Mystery

Candor alert: I'm going to try to explain something that in a sense is inexplicable and incomprehensible. The simple reason the Trinity is a mystery is that it is about God, and God Himself is a mystery. Paul made this observation in another letter:

> By common confession, great is the
>     mystery of godliness:
> He who was revealed in the flesh,
> Was vindicated in the Spirit,
> Seen by angels,
> Proclaimed among the nations,
> Believed on in the world,
> Taken up in glory.[6]

Paul says God cannot be reduced to human logic. We are finite. God is infinite. The finite can never fully understand the infinite. Yes, we should try to understand all of God that we can, but we will never understand everything about God. God Himself said through the prophet Isaiah:

> "For my thoughts are not your thoughts,
>     neither are your ways my ways," declares the LORD.
> "As the heavens are higher than the earth,
>     so are my ways higher than your ways,
>     and my thoughts than your thoughts."[7]

There are two things that the human mind cannot fully understand or comprehend. One is *infinity*; the other is *eternity*. Infinity has no beginning. Eternity has no ending. Yet we know that God is both infinite and eternal. He has neither beginning nor ending. Truly that is incomprehensible because everything we know and see has a beginning and an ending.

Yet some simple observations tell us God has left clues throughout this universe of His Trinitarian nature. For example, the universe is made up of space, matter, and time. Space is height, width, and depth. Matter is energy, motion, and phenomena. Time is past, present, and future. We see it even in ourselves. A person is body, soul, and spirit. Likewise, God is Father, Son, and Holy Spirit.

On the other hand, another reason it is so hard to comprehend the Trinity is that nothing in our world can adequately compare to it. All analogies to the Trinity break down at some point. The Triune God cannot be compared to anything or anyone because God is incomparable.

You can compare one football player with another, one singer with another, one actor with another because there are many of them. But you cannot compare God to any other god because there is no other God except the one God. The prophet Isaiah said: "With whom, then, will you compare God? To what image will you liken him?"[8]

The infinite will not fit into the finite. I confess freely that I don't pretend to understand the Trinity completely.[9] I do agree, however, with the person who said, "Try to define the Trinity, and you'll lose your mind; but choose to deny the Trinity, and you will lose your soul."[10]

## The One Truth Comes in Threes

The word *Trinity* comes from the Latin *trinitas*, which means "a group of three." The three major world religions, Islam, Judaism, and Christianity, agree on one thing: *there is One God.* We hear this over and over again in Scripture.

"I am the LORD, and there is no other;
apart from me there is no God."[11]

For there is one God and one mediator between
God and mankind, the man Christ Jesus.[12]

Christianity is not a polytheistic faith. Christian orthodoxy does not hold to many Gods, nor is it tritheistic—believing in three Gods.

There is only one God, and according to the Bible, God is Trinitarian in nature.

A second truth the Bible teaches about God's nature is that even though only one God exists, *God is also three persons.* We see a hint of this in the very first verse in the Bible.: "In the beginning God created the heavens and the earth."[13]

The Hebrew word used here for God is *Elohim,* which is a plural noun. The suffix *im* in Hebrew gives the singular noun a plural form. A cherub is one angel; cherubim are several angels. A seraph is one angel; seraphim are several angels. *El* is God singular; *Elohim* is gods plural.

However, the verb in this verse ("created") is singular and not plural. Any grammarian would tell you that to couple a plural noun with a singular verb is unacceptable. But the Master Grammarian can suspend the rules when He is sending a theological message. The plural noun *God* coupled with the singular verb *created* indicates that God, though plural in form, is one being.

You see the same thing a few verses later in Genesis 1: "Then God said, 'Let us make mankind in our image, in our likeness.'"[14] Here God is referred to in the plural sense ("us," "our"), but in the next verse we read: "So God [*Elohim*] created mankind in his own image."[15] "Our" refers to God's plurality, and "his" refers to God's singularity.

This phenomenon is what is known as the "plural of majesty." When the Queen of England speaks, she does not use the first person singular; she uses the first person plural. She does not say, "I am happy to be here." She says, "We are happy to be here." Though she is one person, in one sense she is more than one—she represents the entire nation. At the creation, all of the Godhead was present—the Father, Son, and Holy Spirit.

Keep in mind that the bedrock principle of Judaism is what is called the Shema: "Hear, O Israel: The LORD our God, the LORD is one."[16]

The Hebrew word *echad*, translated "one," is a fascinating word that means "one in multiple." It was used to refer to one as in a cluster of grapes.[17] The word as used in the Shema conveys the idea of the Trinity. In fact, think about the word *Trinity*. The prefix *tri* means three; *uni* means one; *tri-unity* means three in one.[18]

---

God is "one What" and "three Whos."

---

It is here that we must be clear on what the Trinity is—and what it is not. *First, the Trinity refers to the fact that there is both a threeness to God and a oneness to God.* We see the "tri" part of God in the various Trinitarian baptism formulas and events[19] while we see the "uni" part of God in the dogmatic declarations that there is one God.[20]

Furthermore, *God is one in His being but three in His personhood.* God is one God, not three, and nowhere does the Bible teach anything else. Nor do orthodox Christians believe in three different Gods. In terms of what God is (substance or being), God is one; in terms of who God is (personhood or subsistence), God is three. One writer put it this way: God is "one What" and "three Whos."[21]

At the same time, each person in the godhead is distinct from the other person. The Father is not the Son and the Son is not the Spirit. Neither the Son nor the Spirit is the Father. To say "Jesus is God" is not identical to the statement "God is Jesus." Jesus is God in that He possesses the same divine nature as the Father and the Spirit. All three persons of the Godhead can properly be described as God, but the three persons are not identical.[22]

Still, though there are three persons in the Godhead and all three are distinct, God is one. In a sense, space is like that. Space is height, width, and depth. If you want to know the total space in a room, you don't add height and width and depth, you multiply height and width and depth. That is the way it is with God. The triune God that we worship is not three Gods, nor is He one God in three parts. He is one God in three persons.

That leads to a third truth: *Each person in the Trinity is fully God.* When we talk about the Trinity, we usually speak of the Father, the Son, and the Holy Spirit, but the Bible sometimes interchanges that order.

Twelve places in the New Testament the three names are grouped together. They are arranged in six different ways, and each of the three names occupies each of the three places twice. The order in which they are placed isn't sacred. None of the persons in the Godhead are either inferior or superior to the others.[23]

In the Old Testament, the one true God is referred to explicitly as "the Lord": "so that all the peoples of the earth may know that the LORD is God and that there is no other."[24] But then in the New Testament we read this declaration:

> Therefore God exalted [Jesus] to the highest place
>     and gave him the name that is above every name,
>   that at the name of Jesus every knee should bow,
>       in heaven and on earth and under the earth,
>     and every tongue acknowledge that *Jesus Christ is Lord,*
>       to the glory of God the Father.[25]

Finally, one other being is identified as Lord: "Now the Lord is the Spirit."[26]

So the question then becomes: "Is the Lord *God*? Is the Lord *Jesus*? Is the Lord *the Holy Spirit*?" And the answer is—yes.

Furthermore, nobody disputes that the one called Father in the New Testament is God, as Jesus Himself made plain.[27] Yet we are told that believers should be looking for "the appearing of the glory of our great God and Savior, Jesus Christ."[28]

Then in the book of Acts, no less than Peter, who spent three years with the man he came to worship as God, clearly identifies the Holy Spirit as God when he confronts a man who had lied about an offering he had given to the church:

> Then Peter said, "Ananias, how is it that Satan has so filled your heart that you have lied to the Holy Spirit and have kept for yourself some of the money you received for the land? Didn't it belong to you before it was sold? And after it was sold, wasn't the money at your disposal? What made you think of doing such a thing? You have not lied just to human beings *but to God.*"[29]

The Bible clearly proclaims that all three persons of the Trinity—God the Father, God the Son, and God the Holy Spirit—are fully God.

---

Without the Trinity there would be no salvation,
and no one would ever come to know God.
In salvation, each member of the Godhead plays
a vital part, and every part is necessary.

---

Ask any child raised in church, "Who created this world?" and the likely answer would be God, with the first verse in the Bible cited as support for that answer. Yet elsewhere in the Bible, these words were written referring to Jesus: "For in him all things were created: things in heaven and on earth, visible and invisible...all things have been created through him and for him."[30] But we are told earlier in the biblical narrative, "His Spirit made the heavens beautiful."[31]

So who created this planet and those who inhabit it? Who made the heavens? Who created the stars and the sun? God did—that is, God the Father, God the Son, and God the Holy Spirit.

## Trinity Ministry

The primary responsibility of the church, according to Jesus Christ Himself, is to carry out the Great Commission, which is to go and make disciples of all the nations and bring people to a saving knowledge of God. So what does the Trinity have to do with this? *Without the Trinity there would be no salvation, and no one would ever come to know God.* In salvation, each member of the Godhead plays a vital part, and every part is necessary for salvation to be accomplished.

---

I do not fully understand the Trinity. But I know God is a Father who loves us; He is a Son who died for us; He is a Spirit who lives within us.

---

Each person in the Trinity plays a unique role in the salvation of all sinners. For example, God the Father *thought* our salvation: "Praise be to the God and Father of our Lord Jesus Christ, who has blessed us in the heavenly realms with every spiritual blessing in Christ. For he chose us in him before the creation of the world to be holy and blameless in his sight."[32] The salvation of the world was in the mind of God the Father before the world came into existence or sin came into the world.

We are then shown how God the Son *bought* our salvation: "In him we have redemption through his blood, the forgiveness of sins, in accordance with the riches of God's grace that he lavished on us."[33] God the Son, obeying God the Father, left heaven and shed His blood and died on the cross so we might have forgiveness for our sins.

But we would still be powerless to receive this salvation except that God the Holy Spirit *wrought* our salvation: "But when the kindness and love of God our Savior appeared, he saved us, not because of righteous things we had done, but because of his mercy. He saved us through the washing of rebirth and renewal by the Holy Spirit."[34]

In order to receive salvation, we must be born again so that we will repent and trust Christ. We cannot do this on our own power—it is the result of the inner working of God the Spirit who leads us to repentance and regenerates our deadened hearts.[35]

One other passage clearly reinforces how the Trinity is linked together in the work of redeeming a world without God: "Peter, an apostle of Jesus Christ, to God's elect...who have been chosen according to the foreknowledge of God the Father, through the sanctifying work of the Spirit, to be obedient to Jesus Christ and sprinkled with his blood."[36]

God the Father *selects* those who will believe, God the Son *saves* those who do believe, and God the Holy Spirit *sanctifies* those who have believed. This is truly teamwork at its ultimate, eternal best. Salvation from first to last is inextricably woven into the fabric of the Trinity.

## The Trinity in a Nutshell

We covered a lot of ground in this chapter, so I offer below five statements that will help you quickly grasp what the Bible says about the Trinity. The Bible affirms the truth of each of these points. Though we may not be able to fully comprehend how all five can be true, this is what the Bible declares about the Trinitarian nature of God. Taken together, these five truths form the essence of the doctrine of the Trinity:

1. The Father is fully God.[37]
2. Jesus is fully God.[38]
3. The Holy Spirit is fully God.[39]
4. These three are distinct persons.[40]
5. There is only one God.[41]

The question is, will we accept God as He reveals Himself in all His mysterious Trinitarian form, or will we only allow a concept of God that we think we can more easily comprehend?[42] The answer to that question has nothing short of eternal consequences.

I admit I do not fully understand the Trinity. But I know God is a Father who loves us; He is a Son who died for us; He is a Spirit who lives within us. For that God, I am eternally thankful.

# CHAPTER THREE

# Did You Use Evolution to Create the Universe?

Over the course of my ministry, one question has bubbled up repeatedly in various settings and on numerous occasions. It has been asked by more skeptics than I care to count and can even come from the unlikeliest of sources.

I am having discussions right now with a young man I will call Sam. He grew up in a strong Christian home with parents who are dedicated Christ-followers. He was baptized under my ministry and served the church in various capacities alongside his parents. When his mom asked me one day to meet with him, I asked why. She looked at the floor and said tearfully, "I would rather he tell you." I sensed her embarrassment and agreed to set up a meeting.

A few days later, Sam sat in my office and blurted out to me his doubts about the whole "God-thing." I listened for a while trying to get my bearings as I was expecting anything but this from a young man I had known practically from infancy. Slowly, I began to peel away the layers until I got to the core of his inquiry: "With all the evidence for evolution, how can you believe in creation? It seems as if we really are accidents who just randomly happened in a universe seemingly out of control."

I commended him for asking a question that has been asked for hundreds of years. In one sense, it is the ultimate question of all: How did the universe come into existence? Furthermore, *why* does it exist?[1]

---

Cheerleaders for evolution and critics
of creationism alike give no quarter on even
allowing for the possibility of an alternative
to their naturalistic dogma.

---

To that seemingly complex question, an incredibly simple answer consisting of ten words comes from the very first verse in the Bible: "In the beginning God created the heavens and the earth."[2]

I admit that many parts of the Bible are difficult to understand and interpret. This is not one of them. The Bible plainly states that behind the entire creative order is God's divine hand. No natural forces exist on their own. Nothing receives its nature or existence from any other source.

Everything that exists bears the handiwork of a divine creator who leaves nothing to chance. These words declare that a distinct plan and a divine purpose are the twin foundations supporting everything, both animate and inanimate.

I realize everything I have just said is hotly debated and derided from hallowed hallways of Ivy League universities to common classrooms in your local high school. Entangled in its web are scientists, doctors, lawyers, judges, teachers, and politicians. Millions of dollars in attorneys' fees have been spent in this culture clash that has reached even the Supreme Court.

A federal judge ruled not long ago that a local school board here in Atlanta could not put stickers on their science textbook with the following statement: "This textbook contains material on evolution. Evolution is a theory, not a fact, regarding the origin of living things. This material should be approached with an open mind, studied carefully and critically considered."[3]

Though that statement seems innocuous at first glance, cheerleaders for evolution and critics of creationism alike give no quarter on even allowing for the possibility of an alternative to their naturalistic dogma. No need for discussion or dialogue, much less debate. The predominant viewpoint among the media, the academy, and even the government will not admit anything that smacks of any direct divine involvement in this world coming into existence.

---

The question remains the same for both believers and nonbelievers: "So how did this universe get here?" I confess I cannot prove creation nor disprove evolution.

---

The question remains the same for both believers and nonbelievers: "So how did this universe get here?" I confess I cannot prove creation nor disprove evolution. Neither one can *definitively* be proved or disproved, for no event that took place when no one was present can be.

All one can do is examine the evidence and, as objectively as possible, decide where the evidence points. I am going to answer this question with six other questions that I hope will lead us to the best answer possible.

## Evolution: What Do You Mean by It?

The first problem in discussing evolution is *defining* evolution. Depending on the definition, one may not have a problem with the word *evolution*. When textbooks say something like, "evolution has occurred," sometimes they just mean that "change sometimes happens." Nobody disagrees with that statement. Certain kinds of limited change do occur in nature.

There are really two meanings to *evolution*. Sometimes the word refers to *micro*evolution, which describes the change that takes place within certain plants and animals over time, but never in a species-altering way. It also specifies certain varieties within different species. That kind of evolution is totally compatible with the Genesis account:

> Then God said, "Let the earth produce every sort of animal, each producing offspring of the same kind—livestock, small animals that scurry along the ground, and wild animals." And that is what happened. God made all sorts of wild animals, livestock, and small animals, each able to reproduce offspring of the same kind.[4]

At other times the term refers to *macro*evolution, and this is where the wheels begin to fall off. This is the theory that made Charles Darwin famous. In essence, Darwin hypothesized that not only did living matter evolve from dead matter through a random process plus time, but that all animals and plants and people evolved from a common ancestor, through a random process of natural selection that ensures the survival of the fittest.

Carl Sagan, the twentieth-century high priest of the religion of evolution, put it this way: "All living things arise by blind physical and chemical forces over eons from slime…and…human beings [and all the other species] have slowly evolved by natural processes from a succession of more ancient beings with no divine intervention needed along the way."[5]

In simple terms, basically Sagan was calling the process by which every living thing came into existence "Explosions-R-Us."

So to recap, "*evolution*" is used in two ways. One word use applies to *limited variation within an existing species,* which nobody denies. The second word use refers to *unlimited change leading to the existence of new groups from one species to another,* which, as will be noted in a moment, is at best highly debatable, and at worst totally speculative. The great debate is over macroevolution, not microevolution.

## Evolution/Creation: Why Does It Matter?

Both the nature and parameters of the creation-evolution debate must be understood. Again, nobody disagrees that natural selection can turn small horses into big horses and small bird beaks into longer bird beaks. But disagreement rages over whether it can turn fish into frogs and frogs into princes. Furthermore, there is not one shred of scientific proof that life ever has or can come from nonlife.

But the question arises, why should creation (a "religious" perspective) be in the arena with evolution (a "scientific" perspective)?

---

The debate is not between fact and faith. The debate is not between science and religion. The debate is between the scientific evidence for evolution and the scientific evidence for creation/design.

---

I contend this is a false perspective. Evolutionary theory and intelligent design theory are not about different subjects; it is not science versus religion. Instead, both are trying to give an answer to the same question: How did the universe and life within it arise? Contrary to an oft-presented caricature of this debate, both perspectives deserve an honest, objective look at the evidence. Which theory best fits the facts? Genesis 1:1, which states that behind this universe is a divine designer, deserves to be put to the test just as much as the theory of evolution.

The debate is not between fact and faith. The debate is not between science and religion. The debate is between the scientific evidence for evolution and the scientific evidence for creation/design. More to the point, it is a debate between two faiths—faith in evolutionary theory and faith in creation/design theory.

This is not the wishful thinking of an uninformed theologian. This is the view even of some on the evolutionary side. Dr. L. Harrison Matthews, a noted evolutionist who wrote the introduction to the 1971 edition of Darwin's famous book *Origin of the Species*, said,

> The fact of evolution is the backbone of biology and biology is thus in the peculiar position of being a science founded on an unproved theory—is it then a science or faith? Belief in the theory of evolution is thus exactly parallel to belief in special creation—both are concepts which believers know to be true, but neither, up to the present, has been capable of proof.[6]

Many evolutionary scientists candidly admit that evolution is based upon belief in the reality of things never seen or scientifically verified—belief in fossils that cannot be produced, in embryological evidence that does not exist, and in breeding experiments that have never worked.[7]

Any objective observer has to conclude that whether you believe in the creation/design worldview or the evolutionary worldview, you have to have faith because there is no absolute verifiable certainty. The issue is not science versus faith. The issue is evolutionary theory versus creation/design theory—all based on the scientific evidence. To pay a backhanded compliment, I believe it takes far more faith to believe in evolution than it does to believe in divine design, as you are going to see in a moment.

In one sense the debate turns on one central fact. If scientists can demonstrate, based on the evidence, that life has emerged purely through natural chemical processes, then God isn't necessary. If, however, the evidence points to a divine design, then the evolutionary house of cards collapses.

The debate is important for every human being who has ever lived, for this reason: Either we were created for a purpose or we are accidental happenings with no discernible purpose for our existence. Either our lives are fulfilling some meaningful plan or our lives have no rhyme or reason. Either some things are universally right or wrong (because a divine lawgiver tells us so) or right and wrong are up for majority vote. All the above turn on which viewpoint prevails.

## Evolution: What Is the Problem?

There are really two basic questions to ask about evolution:

1. Could evolution happen?
2. Did evolution happen?[8]

Let's take the second one first. I see two problems with the question, "Did evolution happen?" The first is what I call the "fossil flaw." If every living being descended from a common ancestor, and people and animals were not separately created, then you would expect to find in ancient fossils thousands of intermediate forms of creatures that have some characteristics of one species and some characteristics of another species. For example, if it is true that a fish eventually turned into a bird, then you would expect to find half-fish/half-bird fossils. But this is exactly where Darwin himself saw the biggest problem: "Innumerable transitional forms must have existed. But why do we not find them imbedded in countless numbers of the crust of the earth?"[9] Darwin himself hoped that in due time these fossils would be found.

As of the twenty-first century, the fossil record is so anti-Darwinian that the evolutionists have had to conjecture that evolution occurs in small groups that evidently were never fossilized. One leading fossil expert put it this way, "Evolution always seems to happen somewhere else."[10]

I remember as a high school student hearing about the "missing link." Yet today the problem is not the missing link—rather, *no chain can be found*. A gap as wide as ever yawns between the evidence for transitional species and the conjecture of the evolutionist. Everybody is waiting for the gap to be filled, but no fill-in has been found.

The second problem with the question is what I call the "dead/life dilemma." No scientific evidence exists that life did (or can) evolve into existence from nonliving matter. Spontaneous generation is still purely speculative from a scientific viewpoint. During all recorded human history, there has never been a substantiated case of a living thing being produced from anything other than another living thing. Every living thing on this planet today had a living, breathing parent. Darwin tried to explain the *survival* of the fittest, but he still can't explain the *arrival* of the fittest.

But what about the first question, "Could evolution happen?" In response to that question, consider three letters—DNA. Within each cell of your body, the chromosomes are couched inside a nucleus. Within the chromosomes is a structure called DNA. DNA is a supermolecule that stores coded hereditary information. It is made up of two long chains of chemical building blocks paired together.

To understand DNA, think of a computer program. It stores and transfers encoded information and instructions. Likewise, the DNA of one human being stores enough encoded information to fill one thousand books, each with five hundred pages of small, closely printed type. This information is far more sophisticated than that of any computer software.

Scientists are beginning to realize that cells containing such a complex code and such intricate chemistry could never have come into being by chance. No matter how chemicals are mixed, they do not create DNA or any intelligent code. Only DNA reproduces DNA.

Sir Fred Hoyle, an internationally recognized astronomer and mathematician and one of Great Britain's foremost scientists, said that the chance of life coming from nonlife is about 10 followed by 40 zeros. What does that mean? Hoyle says, "There is about as much chance of life being spontaneously produced as there is a tornado blowing through a junkyard and building a Boeing 747."[11]

## Evolution: Why Such Scientific Devotion?

A legitimate question arises at this point: If evolution is such a deficient theory—if in fact it is a theory with many inherent weaknesses, as I contend—why do so many scientists so vigorously defend it? One glaring reason is the faith of the evolutionist gets in the way of the facts of science. One of the most famous modern-day evolutionary proponents, Richard Dawkins, made this glaring admission: "*Even if there were no actual evidence* in favor of the Darwinian theory...we should still be justified in preferring it over all rival theories."[12]

I give Dawkins credit. He was just expressing the sentiment of much of the scientific community: "My mind is made up; don't confuse me with the facts."

But why such stubborn dogmatism? Why the refusal to even consider any other possibility for the existence of all things apart from an evolutionary explanation?

Again, let's listen to another prominent member of the scientific community. George Wald, former professor of biology at Harvard University and a 1967 Nobel Prize winner in physiology, admitted:

> There are only two possibilities as to how life arose: one is spontaneous generation arising to evolution. The other is a supernatural creative act of God. There is no third possibility. Spontaneous generation, the belief that life comes from non-living matter, was scientifically disproved a hundred and twenty years ago by Louis Pasteur and others. That just leaves us with only one other possibility...that life arose as a creative act of God. But, I will not accept that philosophy, because I do not want to believe in God, therefore, I choose to believe in that which I know is scientifically impossible, spontaneous generation leading to evolution.[13]

Harvard biologist Richard Lewontin, even while admitting the "patent absurdity" of much evolutionary theory, said simply, "We cannot allow a divine foot in the door."[14] I call this the ABG mentality—Anything But God.

---

When God loses His preeminence,
man loses his significance.

---

So the dirty secret is exposed. Evolution is more than just science. It is both a philosophy and a kind of faith. It is a philosophy that says, "This is a closed universe and the supernatural does not exist." It is a faith that has Darwin as its prophet, *Origin of the Species* as its Bible, and the theory of evolution as its god.

## Evolution: Why Is Believing It So Harmful?

So what if people still want to believe in the theory? What is the harm? Think about it. Either we are the accidental by-product of a random, purposeless process or we have been created in God's image with a purpose, by His design. If we are the by-product of time, chance, and random processes, then regardless of what else one says, it is difficult to determine what if anything is unique about life, human or animal. What exactly gives human life any intrinsic worth? But if we are a creation of a God who made us in His image, that is a game changer.

Much of the so-called "culture of death" in our society has as its underlying cause the teaching of evolution. Do not be oblivious to the connection between those who advocate an unfettered right to abortion and the economic necessity of euthanasia with the evolutionary mind-set. That is why some have called evolution, "the big lie."

This "big lie" leads us to devastating conclusions if carefully thought through. Evolutionist William Provine of Cornell University honestly admits that if evolution is true, there are five inescapable conclusions:

- There is no evidence for God—and no need for God.
- There is no life after death.
- There is no absolute foundation for right and wrong.
- There is no ultimate meaning to life.
- People don't really have free will.[15]

We see the real problem with this dangerous belief: *When God loses His preeminence, man loses his significance.*

I contend that evolution and theism are incompatible. Evolution is dependent on random mutations and natural selection. By definition, random mutations are unguided.[16] Theistic evolutionists maintain that God uses this process to create life and its diversity.

But once God is involved, intelligence and design must come into play, and an intelligent being cannot use *random* mutations. The selection would be supernaturally controlled, not naturally produced. The words *random* and *natural* are meant to exclude both intelligence and design—two qualities inherent in this magnificent universe. If God guides the mutations, they are not *random;* if God chooses which organisms survive through mutations, the process is *supernatural* (intelligent) rather than *natural*.[17] One cannot have his cake and eat it too.

This is a battle over more than just science, for this philosophical view inevitably bleeds over to ethics, law, education, morality, and the sanctity of life (born and unborn). It is like a cancer in the bloodstream that affects every vital organ of our culture.

## Creation/Design: Why Is Believing It Such a Big Deal?

One of the most memorable experiences of my life took place on Hawaii's Big Island. My wife and I were celebrating our twentieth wedding anniversary. We had been told of a restaurant that was right on the ocean. I visited the restaurant the day before and noticed one table was set apart from the others and jutted out toward the ocean. I am not the greatest romantic in the world, but I knew I had to have that table.

I met with the maître d' and asked for that table to be reserved. I also made sure our reservation would be close to the time when the sun would set. I could hardly wait for the time to arrive so Teresa would see how thoughtful I had been.

When we arrived, the waiter escorted us to our special table. I didn't realize what a coup I had pulled off until we sat down. As we watched that golden globe slowly dissolve in the distance, I noticed two palm trees that had grown together forming a V. My sweetheart and I watched in silent rapture as the trees swayed in the wind, the ukuleles played, and the sun went down right between the V. Steven Spielberg couldn't have done it any better.

I watched that sun sink beneath the horizon as whales breached and the surf crashed against the shore just a few feet from us. Unlike the evolutionist, who sees nothing except the fortuitous result of random processes, I could not help but think of the words of the psalmist:

> The heavens declare the glory of God;
>     the skies proclaim the work of his hands.[18]

The Bible makes no bones about it. This earth was divinely designed. The heavens "declare" and "proclaim" the reality of both its divine design and its divine designer. If you can't hear its clarion call, the problem is spiritual deafness, not lack of evidence. If you look at this creation and don't see evidence of a Creator, don't blame the Creator. Don't blame the watchmaker if you don't see him behind the watch. Don't blame the artist if you don't see him behind the portrait. Don't blame the photographer if you don't see him behind the picture.

It is *the* question of all questions: Is this planet just an accident? Is it accidental that the inexhaustible envelope of air only fifty miles deep has exactly the right density to support human life? Is it accidental that unlike other substances, water expands when it freezes, which makes ice float on the surface of lakes and prevents them from freezing solid and allows the fish to survive? Is it accidental that the earth tilts so that most of the planet enjoys four different seasons? Is it accidental that the sun's fire does not generate so much heat that we fry, but just enough that we don't freeze?

Is the force of gravity just blind luck? If it were slightly stronger, all stars would be blue cold instead of white hot, unable to support life. If slightly weaker, all stars would burn too rapidly for life to develop. Cosmologists muse about "cosmic coincidences"—meaning that the fundamental forces of the universe just *happen* to mesh together in such a way that makes life possible. Even the slightest variation would mean life in the universe would be impossible.[19]

Go to a mirror and look into your own eyes. Those eyes need about

130 million light-sensitive devices to cause a photochemical reaction that transforms light into electrical impulses that go to the brain. Every second, 1000 million of those impulses are zipped to the brain through the optical nerve system. Your eye can handle 1.5 million simultaneous messages. When exposed to darkness, it can increase its ability to see by 100,000 times and 137 million nerve endings pick up every message the eye sends to the brain.

> We are not a chance collection of atoms and molecules that just happened to come together by fate. The God who created all things for our enjoyment and for His praise and glory made us.

Are the intricacies of this universe and the human body just the result of blind evolutionary chance? Is it really "In the beginning nothing" or "In the beginning God"? As someone once put it, "If you came into the kitchen and saw the alphabet cereal spilled on the table and it spelled out your name and address, would you think the cat knocked the cereal box over?" Those who don't hold to the "cat theory" have every right to ask, "Where does the evidence lead?"

Anthony Flew, a British philosophy professor, had been a leading champion of atheism for more than a half century and once debated C.S. Lewis on the existence of God. Before his death, after decades of insisting that belief in God was ridiculous, he changed his mind and concluded that based on scientific evidence, there had to be a super-intelligence, a first-cause, as the only good explanation for the origin of life and the complexity of nature.

Much to the chagrin of his erstwhile scientific friends and colleagues, Dr. Flew finally had to acknowledge that the overwhelming evidence for Intelligent Design destroys the theory of evolution. It takes out chance and it puts in God. That is why the evolutionist hates the theory of creation/design so much.

Let me make this super-personal to everyone reading these words. *Only when you understand **how** you got here will you ever understand **why** you are here.* Only God as creator can provide satisfying answers to the basic questions of human existence. Questions and answers such as:

- Where did I come from?
  I came from the heart and mind of an omnipotent, omniscient God who has a plan for my life.

- Who am I?
  I am the highest of all God's creation, put here by a God who desires to have a personal relationship with me.

- Why am I here?
  I am here to know that God, to love that God, to serve that God, and to fulfill His plan for my life.

- How should I live?
  I should live according to the commandments He has given me in His Word, so that I can fulfill His will for my life.

- What is my destiny?
  A life of faithfulness here and an eternity spent in the presence of the One who made me for His glory awaits me if I have a personal relationship with Him through His Son, Jesus Christ.

We are not a chance collection of atoms and molecules that just happened to come together by fate. We are not the result of some cosmic lottery. The God who created all things for our enjoyment and for His praise and glory made us. That is a truth supported not only by scientific evidence, but spoken by the God who created all science and who cannot lie.

CHAPTER FOUR

# If You're So Good, Why Do You Allow Innocents to Suffer?

W hat is the meaning of it, Watson?" said Holmes solemnly as he laid down the paper. "What object is served by this circle of misery and violence and fear? It must tend to some end, or else our universe is ruled by chance, which is unthinkable. But what end? There is the great standing perennial problem to which human reason is as far from an answer as ever.[1]

His name is Tommy. If you look in the dictionary for either "good old boy" or "gentle teddy bear," you might see his picture. Tommy is good folk from Mayberry, Mr. Nice Guy, a sweet giant of a man who could break most people in half and yet wouldn't hurt a fly. He is, as the older President Bush would have put it, a "kinder, gentler" American you would love to have for your next-door neighbor, a middle-aged man who would get your mail and watch your house if you were out of town. But beneath this seemingly idyllic veneer lay a heart that had been crushed by one of the saddest stories I have ever heard.

We were riding on a bus through the Israeli countryside between biblical sites, and even though Tommy attended our church, we had never had a one-on-one conversation. He was sitting next to his precious wife, Beth, and I casually asked how long they had been married. When he said "eight months," I guess the surprised look on my face was obvious (reason number thirty-five why I have never played poker). With no further prompting, he spilled out his story like a waterfall in fast forward.

> "I just couldn't understand how God could allow something like this. I had been living for Him, serving Him, and now my life was destroyed."

Tommy married his first wife in the early seventies with rock solid "till death do you part" commitment—at least on his part. He discovered just two years into the marriage that she was involved with another man, and he was devastated. He intended to divorce her, but she asked for forgiveness and a second chance. After counseling, he agreed and took her back only to learn that she was pregnant. There was reason to doubt that the child was his, but Tommy was determined to do the right thing. Soon a son was born and then a daughter.

The marriage seemed to stabilize, but a few years later Tommy came home from work to find his wife and children gone. No note, no letter, nothing. For two weeks he could not even locate his family; then divorce papers arrived in the mail. His wife was asking for the home, child support, and alimony, even though Tommy had been a model husband and father. He also discovered that his wife had been involved in another affair that had been going on for over a year. Looking out the bus window as the Jerusalem countryside rolled by, Tommy tearfully said, "I just couldn't understand how God could allow something like this. I had been living for Him, serving Him, and now my life was destroyed. Once again, I was devastated." I was beginning to regret I had even started this conversation, it was so depressing.

Then the story seemed to turn for the better. Tommy countersued for custody of his children (even his soon to be ex-wife's sister testified in his behalf), and in a rare occurrence, Tommy was granted full custody. *Hmmm...maybe God does get it right after all*, he thought. For two years he and his children enjoyed the happiest times of their lives, and then things got better. Tommy met a wonderful lady with two children of her own, and they soon fell in love. All the children were happy with the other potential new parent, and soon Tommy and Carly were married. Carly's and Tommy's daughters became best friends, and her children became just like his own. It was truly a Brady Bunch dream come true. Eleven years of idyllic family life and marital bliss followed, but the "happily ever after" glass was again to be shattered with the hammer of another unbelievable tragedy.

Tommy received a call from his cousin, who worked in the emergency room at the local hospital. "Isn't Carly's son named Mark?"

"Yes."

"You better get Carly and get down here immediately, but Tommy, you need to know...it's too late."

Tommy called Carly's supervisor where she worked and asked him to have her meet him at the front door in thirty minutes because of an emergency. As he drove to pick her up, all he could ask God was, "How do I tell my wife that her thirty-two-year-old son is dead?" He chose to say as little as possible, pleading ignorance.

A chaplain and two homicide detectives met them. Tommy was

asked to go in and identify the body, which had been brutalized and mutilated by sixteen stab wounds. He then had to watch his wife throw herself over the cold, lifeless body of her son and wail uncontrollably. With more tears flowing, Tommy looked at me and said, "Carly died that moment with a broken heart—it just took another four agonizing years to realize it." I had a sinking feeling that this story still hadn't hit bottom.

Carly fell into a deep depression, which moved both her and Tommy into an early retirement. She retired because she was so emotionally crippled she could no longer work, and he retired to give her full-time care. Through trembling lips, Tommy said, "Carly withdrew into a world of depression, heartache, and pain." After a pause to gather himself, he blurted out, "I felt God had totally abandoned us."

Carly withdrew into "the world of Mark." She placed the urn containing his ashes in her china cabinet surrounded by pictures of him. She became obsessed with this shrine. She had a cross made that contained some of his ashes and placed it on a necklace she wore 24/7. Every day she would go the china cabinet and talk to the urn and cry uncontrollably. Every night she would fall asleep crying in Tommy's arms.

"My world was caving in on me slowly but surely," Tommy told me. "Doctors put her on every kind of antidepressant medicine available, but they only seemed to make things worse. We prayed constantly to God, but it seemed as if our prayers fell on deaf ears."

Carly spent $3,000 on cement statues and a small headstone and built another shrine for Mike in their backyard. Finally, she insisted on buying a plot for a headstone in a cemetery to further honor his memory.

Then came the trial.

The jury refused to render a verdict for murder, downgrading the crime to manslaughter, and Mark's killer was given a seven-year term but only had to serve two because of a quirky Alabama law. Carly sank even deeper into her personal bog of despair.

Then what Tommy had feared came to pass: Carly overdosed on enough medication to kill at least ten people, the doctors told him later after he had rushed her to the hospital where she was admitted in a deep coma. Tommy was also told there was little hope that she would ever regain consciousness, and if she did, she would either be in a vegetative state or her organs would shut down.

What would you have done at this point? To my astonishment, Tommy recounted how he found a Gideon Bible and began to pray over Carly and read Scripture to her. "I read and prayed nonstop for hours until I was completely hoarse. *God, I don't know where You have been or why all this has happened to me, but I know You are still God, and right now I need a miracle.*" At that point, Tommy smiled for the first time in this now seemingly endless chorus of sadness and said, "At that moment, she squeezed my hand, opened her eyes, and wanted to know where she was." I allowed myself to think at this point "*now* they live happily ever after." I wish.

Carly immediately became upset and violently angry because she had survived. To Tommy's relief, the doctors recommended that she be admitted to a psychiatric hospital for treatment. Finally, the medical cavalry had arrived to lend aid to a man at the end of his emotional rope.

He wished.

After only six days, Tommy got a call from a social worker asking if he was ready to bring his wife home. Frantically, Tommy called the doctor in charge of Carol's case, and he assured Tommy that after talking to Carly, she understood how foolish she had been and how determined she was to live a new, productive life.

"I begged the doctor to reconsider. I told him that Carly had been a psychiatric nurse for twenty-two years, and she knew how to play the game."

His plea fell on deaf ears, and Tommy reluctantly picked her up after making her "swear in the name of Jesus Christ" she would never try to harm herself again.

Three days later they celebrated Carly's fifty-eighth birthday, and she smiled for the first time since the trial—and the last time on this earth. The next four days saw Carly's emotional state completely tank to an unprecedented low. Alarmed, Tommy called the doctor and begged him to have her admitted to the hospital that day, but the doctor instead made an appointment for the following day believing that there was no urgency.

"The next morning as we were preparing to go to the appointment, the dogs were barking outside, and Carly begged me to go and quiet them as they were giving her a tremendous headache. She promised me she would be fine and I would only be gone for a minute. The last part of her assertion was true. I was gone for no more than a minute when I heard a shot ring out. I knew immediately what had happened."

I fought back tears as Tommy went on.

"She had gotten access to a gun without my knowledge. No sooner had I walked out than I heard the gunshot, and at 7:00 a.m. Carly's earthly life was over. All I had fought for was gone. As I waited for the police and the ambulance, my life came crashing down like a ton of bricks. All I could say over and over was, 'How could this happen? Why would God spare her life only to take it a few days later?'"

Looking out the window again, Tommy said, "I told God He had let all of us down; how could He do such a thing? *Why* would He do such a thing? Why give me hope, then snatch it away? Was this some kind of sick cosmic joke?" He then looked at me with grief radiating from his eyes. "When you lose a son it tears at your heart, but when you lose your wife, it tears the heart out of your soul. At my lowest I finally told God, 'You get such pleasure in destroying people's lives, why don't You take mine? You have destroyed all You gave me—are You happy now?'"

---

A Barna poll asked, "If you could ask God only one question, what would you ask?" By far the most common reply was, "Why is there pain and suffering in the world?"

---

I felt the punch to my gut with those words. Even as you read this, you may feel the veins pop out on your neck, your blood pressure rise. *Yeah, if God is so good and God is so powerful, why are there so many Tommys in the world?* It would be one thing if Tommy were a slimy adulterer, a vicious murderer, a child abuser, or a pimp who preyed on young girls. At least there would be some intellectual relief to reason and some emotional relief to the heart. But Tommy truly is a "good ol' boy." Religious. Church-going. God-fearing. Moral. Upright. Do-gooder. You don't have to beg this question; it begs you to answer it: *Why do bad things happen to good people?*

## The Elephant in the Room

This one question causes more unbelief, doubt, or downright rejection of God than any other problem. It's the one and only bullet in the atheist's gun. There are many proofs (or apparent proofs) and arguments for theism, but only one argument dogmatically claims to disprove the existence of God—the existence of evil.[2]

A Barna poll asked, "If you could ask God only one question and you knew He would give you an answer, what would you ask?" By far the most common reply was, "Why is there pain and suffering in the world?"[3] Many pastors will tell you that this question surfaces frequently. In my own life, I have walked with families whose babies were taken in crib deaths, mourned over teenagers killed by drunk drivers, consoled wives-turned-widows through an inexplicable suicide, and fought back confusion in the face of children ravaged by cancer.

Frustrations such as these touch us all, regardless of the strength of one's faith. When you look at a world created and controlled by an all-powerful, all-knowing, all-loving Supreme Being, and you see rivers of evil, pain, and suffering overflowing the banks of every country and continent, you find yourself almost screaming, "What is wrong with this picture?"

---

*No matter how hard you try,
trouble is going to come your way.*

---

Even as I type these words, I hear on the news that two women and two children ages five and three have been found "executed" in Maryland. I thought of my own two-year-old grandson, and before I knew it, I found myself asking, "Oh God, how could You let this happen?"

The eminent teacher and theologian John Stott confesses:

> The fact of suffering undoubtedly constitutes the single greatest challenge to the Christian faith, and has been in every generation. Its distribution and degree appear to be entirely random and therefore unfair. Sensitive spirits ask if it can possibly be reconciled with God's justice and love.[4]

I appreciate Stott's use of the term *sensitive spirits*. It is not just the skeptic or the militant atheist who struggles with this problem. As you will see, some of God's greatest saints and spiritual leaders have also wrestled with this seemingly intractable problem.

The problem actually goes even deeper. Bad things do happen to good people, but bad things also happen to bad people, and at times some even think that bad people get far worse than they deserve. This is one reason many people think no one deserves hell, for example, or they would spare even an Adolf Hitler from capital punishment. Whether you consider yourself a good or bad person, you are going to have to deal with unexplained and (in your mind at least) undeserved evil. No matter how hard you try, trouble is going to come your way.

We understand why bad things happen to bad people. We understand why good things happen to good people. I believe most of us can even live with the fact that good things happen to bad people. But what bothers us most is when bad things happen to good people. It just doesn't seem fair. It is so difficult for many to reconcile this problem with a loving, benevolent, omnipotent God.

It was the skeptic David Hume in 1776 who classically stated the problem in a series of questions about God:

> Is he willing to prevent evil, but not able? Then he is impotent. Is he able, but not willing? Then he is malevolent. Is he both able and willing? Whence then is evil…Why is there any misery at all in the world? Not by chance surely. From some cause then. Is it from the intention of the Deity? But he is perfectly benevolent. Is it contrary to his intention? But he is almighty. *Nothing can shake the solidity of this reasoning, so short, so clear, so decisive.*[5]

Hume's last statement is, to use a sports turn of phrase, "the ball game." Is it really implausible to believe in the biblical God who is love,[6] who can do the impossible,[7] and who wants all things to work out for the good of those who love Him,[8] when there is so much evil, pain, and suffering in the world? Are Christopher Hitchens and Richard Dawkins right in saying the problem of evil sounds the death knell for any rational basis for believing in the God of Abraham, Isaac, and Jacob? If God is so good, why is the world so bad?

The problem of evil is the theological elephant in the room. How do you answer those who see innocent babies killed, young people die of cancer, little children brutalized and murdered, and come to one of two conclusions: Either God doesn't exist or He is not much of a God.

## It's Just Not Fair

It doesn't take long for the world's bestselling book to tackle the problem of evil head on. Barely two chapters into the greatest story ever told evil rears its ugly head, and a perfect world becomes a spiritual Hiroshima. All of a sudden murder, child sacrifice, rape, homosexuality, fornication, and even genocide become the order of the day. The specific term for evil is found six hundred times in Scripture.

This book pulls no punches in facing the reality of evil and especially the problem of the bad happening to the good. Two men in particular raised this question to God, one because of his *observance* and the other because of his *experience*.

The first man was Asaph. We don't know much about him, but according to one of the dozen or so songs he wrote, he was one ticked off minstrel. The title of this psalm might well have been, "I'm Mad as _____, and I Am Not Going to Take It Anymore!" Two things about life really galled him and tore at the fabric of his belief in God. One was the *prosperity of the wicked*:

> For I was envious of the arrogant
>> when I saw the prosperity of the wicked.
> For they have no pangs until death;
>> their bodies are fat and sleek.
> They are not in trouble as others are;
>> they are not stricken like the rest of mankind…

> Behold, these are the wicked;
> always at ease, they increase in riches.[9]

Asaph observed that some of the most wicked, crooked, unspiritual, nonreligious people in the community lived in luxury. They had the Midas touch. They prospered in every way imaginable—physically, financially, and socially. They never got caught. They seemed to get away with everything. Yet he seemingly could handle that oddity because after all God is good, it rains on the just and the unjust, and there is such a thing as "common grace."

But what he *could not* take was the *adversity of the righteous*. How could a loving righteous God allow those who hated Him to prosper while at the same time allowing those who loved Him to suffer unbelievable hurt and trouble? He had experienced a measure of this himself:

> All in vain I have kept my heart clean
> and washed my hands in innocence.
> For all day long I have been stricken
> and rebuked every morning.[10]

Asaph was playing by the rules, doing life by the numbers. His life was as clean as the wicked was corrupt, as committed as they were carnal. "What's the use of living right if God isn't going to do right? I would be better off being a convict then a convert." Such was the bitter complaint of this God-fearing, temple-going, taxpaying good guy. To him this was the one question that perhaps even God couldn't answer, the one action even God couldn't justify.

Of course the poster child for having an undeserved bad day is the patriarch Job. The fascinating saga bearing his name begins by emphasizing the impeccable goodness of this man: "In the land of Uz there lived a man whose name was Job. This man was blameless and upright; he feared God and shunned evil."[11]

The Hebrew word for "shun" means "to turn off." Job was so righteous and good that even the thought of doing anything displeasing to God or dishonorable to himself was a complete turnoff to him. His goodness was off the charts. No skeletons in his closet—not even a bone. The IRS, the CIA, the FBI, and Interpol together couldn't dig up even a teaspoon of dirt in his life.

As if to leave no doubt as to the sterling character of this man, we are told this was not just a human opinion of Job, it was God's: "Then the LORD said to Satan, 'Have you considered my servant Job? There is no one on earth like him; he is blameless and upright, a man who fears God and shuns evil.'"[12]

God himself gives Job's life the "Good Housekeeping Seal" of His approval. If anyone deserved to get all the breaks, it would be this paragon of virtue. From all indications, even the most cynical faultfinders among his peers couldn't find a dent in his public or private life. He is called "the greatest man among all the people of the East."[13]

---

Is there any theological water that can be poured
on these hearts parched by the desert heat of
seemingly insensible pain, heartache, and suffering?

---

Job carried a lot of weight in his community. He was the first E.F. Hutton—when he spoke everyone listened. His name was a household word. Righteous, religious, respected—almost a perfect ten in the eyes of anyone who knew or even heard of him.

So this godly, gracious, generous man lived happily ever after, and God rewarded his goodness with good, right? Hardly. Faster than a speeding bullet Job went from hero to zero. In case you haven't heard, in one day Job lost it all—finances, family (only his wife survived), and fitness as he too was ravaged with painful boils all over his body.[14]

Why? Brace yourself: Because the devil bet God if Job was pummeled with pain and saturated with suffering, he wouldn't be Mr. Wonderful. And God took the wager and let the devil wreak havoc in his life.[15] You heard correctly: Job ran into the buzz saw of suffering, not because he was doing so many things wrong, but because he was doing so many things right.

Today, you don't have to look far to see the world littered with the broken hearts of the Tommys, Asaphs, and Jobs. You are married to them, work with them, attend school with them, live next door to them. The question is, what do you say to them? Is there any theological water that can be poured on these hearts parched by the desert heat of seemingly insensible pain, heartache, and suffering?

## You Talkin' to Me?

Disclaimer: If you are hoping to find the silver bullet that will slay this vampire of unexplained suffering, you are going to be sorely disappointed. There are thousands of books, articles, and essays on theodicy (relax: it means the problem of explaining God's goodness and power in view of the existence of evil), and none to my knowledge claims to have the definitive answer that will assuage all concerns. I believe I know why.

In all of Scripture God never explains why He allows evil and suffering. Interestingly, after the second chapter of Job, we don't hear from God again for thirty-six chapters. After witnessing the supposed "friends" of Job try to explain the problem, God lets Job know in no uncertain terms that *He doesn't owe anyone an explanation for anything He does.*

It is the height of arrogance at worst and the folly of ignorance at best for the finite to question the infinite, for the creation to question the Creator. One question stopped Job dead in his tracks and should stop anyone bent on challenging God to a theological duel:

"Where were you when I laid the earth's foundation?
    Tell me, if you understand.
Who marked off its dimensions? Surely you know!"[16]

Understand this was not simply a smarmy smackdown by God, nor was it a tactic of intimidation. Rather, it was God's way of reminding Job—and us—that a finite perspective of this world in any facet is at best incomplete and at worst utter foolishness. On the one hand, God doesn't have to defend Himself to anyone. On the other hand, even though evil and suffering don't make sense to us, that doesn't mean they don't make sense. Even though the vilest deeds can appear to be arbitrary and random, they are not *precisely because there is a God* who uses them for His eternal purpose and personal glory.

In his magnificent book, *If God Is Good*, Randy Alcorn astutely points out the circular reasoning used in stating the problem of evil. The assumption is that evil and an all-good, all-powerful, all-knowing God cannot coexist. There can be no valid reason that such a God would create such a world.

But Alcorn rightly notes this begs the question. What proof is there that this assumption is correct?[17] How can a finite creature possibly have the perspective of an eternal Creator? Rather, we should affirm that if God exists, He knows far more than we do and is certainly capable of weaving even the seemingly most random unjust acts of suffering and violence into the tapestry of His sovereign purpose.

If God declares He has a morally sufficient reason for permitting evil this would in no way contradict His omnipotence, omniscience, or His loving-kindness.[18] God's ways and thoughts are far above ours.[19] This fact alone should remind us of the limits of our logic and the restrictions of our reason.[20] Just because we cannot see any purpose for evil and suffering does not mean no explanation exists.[21]

## Bridge Over Troubled Waters

Still, we do find in Scripture some clues as to how and why God uses evil and suffering in the lives of both the believer and the unbeliever. We are also reminded why He is God and we are not. This list is not exhaustive and will not substitute for trusting God's purposes and providence even in the most difficult of times, but I do believe they are there to help us maintain a divine perspective on this intractable problem.

First, *without God there can be no true good.* In one sense, it is a misnomer to speak of bad things happening to good people because no human being is totally and completely good. Mark 10 records the story of a rich young man who approached Jesus and asked Him how to inherit eternal life. When he referred to Jesus as "good teacher," Jesus immediately stunned him with a question that went to the core of any human concept of goodness: "Why do you call me good? No one is good—except God alone."[22] God is both the standard by which all goodness must be measured and the epitome of goodness itself.

> Evil does not pose a problem for faith in a loving God as much as it bolsters faith in such a God.

Ironically, the question we are dealing with, far from calling a good God into question, actually demands the existence of one. Without a perfectly good God, who determines what is universally good? Who is to say what good is? What objective basis exists for measuring morality? Without God, good and bad, right and wrong are just matters of personal opinion.

The argument that the existence of evil demands the nonexistence of a good God can actually be flipped to the exact opposite conclusion.

To the skeptic who says, "Since evil exists, God cannot," one could reply, "Since evil exists, God *must also,* for without good there is no evil and without God there is no good."[23] Without God, goodness, morality, and right and wrong are just matters of personal opinion or majority vote.[24]

Ethicist and atheist Richard Taylor concedes, "To say that something is wrong because…it is forbidden by God, is also perfectly understandable to anyone who believes in a law-giving God. But to say that something is wrong…even though no God exists to forbid it, is *not* understandable."[25] Taylor is dead on.

So the first thing to remember is that evil does not pose a problem for faith in a loving God as much as it bolsters faith in such a God.

Second, *we must keep in mind that our knowledge is imperfect and limited; God is omniscient with unlimited and perfect knowledge.* The only way we could know definitively that evil should not exist in a God-created world and that evil in no way could be used for a greater good is to have perfect knowledge of all possible worlds. But we don't even have perfect knowledge of the world we live in.

We must allow for the possibility that God's purpose can best be fulfilled and His glory best displayed in a world where evil and suffering exist.[26] Proverbs 16:4 states categorically:

> The LORD works out everything to its proper end—
> even the wicked for a day of disaster.

Either this world is nothing more than randomness gone wild (which would truly render the question of evil moot anyway) or behind this planet is a divine purpose that can include evil and suffering in its ultimate fulfillment. This truth is seen both in Scripture and in history, as I will demonstrate shortly.

Third, *God can and does use evil and suffering to achieve both a greater good and His personal glory.* God is not just some deus ex machina that faith manufactures to cope with a seemingly intractable problem. Yet without God, there can be neither any purpose behind any evil or suffering nor any final resolution to it. Only a God who can use suffering for a greater purpose can bring meaning to it. Only a God who can use evil for His glory and the ultimate good of others can give assurance that justice will prevail.

God does all things for two reasons: His glory and our good. The order is important, for one flows from the other. God does everything for His sake first. His primary concern is His glory. But anything God does for His glory is always for our benefit. Whatever glorifies God gratifies us. That includes the evil God allows to invade our lives and the suffering He allows to attack our bodies. Two biblical figures illustrate this: Joseph and Jesus.

One-fourth of the book of Genesis is given over to the story of a teenager named Joseph. Fourteen chapters tell the story of a young man who repeatedly got what he didn't deserve. Jealousy drove his brothers to plan his murder, but at the last minute they decided to sell him to some foreign merchants, where he landed in a strange land working as a slave in the household of a man named Potiphar.

Though Joseph soon rose to be Potiphar's most productive and trustworthy employee, his master had him thrown into prison when his wife falsely accused Joseph of trying to rape her. Joseph had actually refused the woman's repeated advances out of his commitment to God and his loyalty to his master. But "hell knows no fury like a woman scorned," and for thirteen years Joseph languished in a dungeon for a crime he didn't commit.

At every turn of his life, Joseph makes the right call, chooses the right path, exercises the right decision, and he still gets burned. He had done nothing to deserve being thrown into a pit, forced into slavery, or hauled off to prison. Nothing but bad things happened to this good person. On the surface, it seems as if a loving, compassionate God is nowhere to be found (even though the story repeatedly states, "the LORD was with Joseph"[27]) or He's incapable of intervening.

But in an incredible turn of events, a former inmate remembered Joseph, and he was brought before Pharaoh, the ruler of all Egypt. In a meeting that lasted about fifteen minutes, Joseph was made the prime minister of Egypt. This promotion eventually allowed Joseph to bring his father, Jacob, and his entire family to Egypt and prevented the demise of what would become the nation of Israel from a worldwide famine.

But before Jacob and his family made the journey to Egypt, Joseph had an incredible meeting with his brothers in which he revealed himself to them and then taught them about God and Evil 101. Seeing all that had happened to him from God's perspective, he said to his brothers, "Do not be distressed and do not be angry with yourselves for selling me here, because it was to save lives that God sent me ahead of you…God sent me ahead of you to preserve for you a remnant on earth and to save your lives by a great deliverance. So then, it was not you that sent me here, but God."[28]

Jaws dropped like the stock market in 1929; eyes widened like a mouth before a hot Krispy Kreme doughnut. Is my hearing all right? Is he serious? No bitterness? No anger? No revenge? Correct, for there is no place for these emotions if a sovereign, loving God is working all things out for His glory and our good—including the evil and suffering inflicted on us by others. God not only *allowed* Joseph to be taken to Egypt, God actually *arranged* for Joseph to be sent there using his brothers' evil deeds.[29]

Later, Joseph put his entire ordeal into perspective when he summed up not just *what* had happened to him but *why*: "As for you, you meant evil against me, but God meant it for good, to bring it about that many people should be kept alive, as they are today."[30] A phrase in this verse is a beacon of light that always shines against the darkness of evil and suffering: "God meant it for good" is always the ultimate end of all evil from an eternal, divine viewpoint.

"God meant it for good" communicates something far stronger than God being handed lemons and making lemonade. God did not merely make the best of a bad situation; fully aware of what Joseph's brothers would do, and fully permitting their sin, God *intended* that the bad situation—which He could have prevented but didn't—be used for good.[31]

## The Greatest Good from the Worst Evil

The greatest and supreme answer to the question about the existence of evil is in the universal symbol of Christianity—the cross. The cross of Christ speaks definitively to a question from New Testament scholar Bart Ehrman, who writes: "I came to think that there is not a God who is actively involved with this world of pain and misery—if he is, why doesn't he do something about it?"[32]

I contend that God *did* do something when He came into this world as a man not immune to evil and suffering but a man "despised and rejected by mankind, a man of suffering, and familiar with pain... he was despised, and we held him in low esteem."[33] Jesus was the only truly *good* person, and bad things happened to Him. He was in fact the only *perfect* person, and He endured the vilest evil and the worst suffering of all time.

Have you ever wondered why we call the Friday before Easter Good Friday? What was good about it? Shouldn't it be called Bad Friday instead?[34] Wasn't it on that day that the inhabitants of earth did their worst to heaven's best? It was the worst crime in history—we killed God's own Son for our own sins.

Who in all of history endured the greatest injustice? The greatest evil? The greatest suffering? Who paid the highest price ever paid for undeserved wickedness, pain, and anguish? The answer is *God*.[35]

Looking at evil and suffering through the prism of the cross is the ultimate game changer. The question changes from "Why did you do this *to* me?" to "Why did you do that *for* me?"[36] It only stands to reason that if God could bring eternal benefits such as salvation, eternal life, forgiveness, and joy through the evil done to Jesus, then He certainly can do the same in our own suffering.

> What we may think are random senseless accidents may serve a greater purpose and effect a greater good. God sees every possible outcome of every possible action, and the cross tells us that we can and must trust His hand to fit all evil and suffering into His glory and our good.

Another sobering thought flows from the river of suffering Christ endured: Imagine the greater evil the human race would have experienced if God had not allowed the greatest evil of all. The greatest good (eternal life and complete forgiveness) would never have occurred, and the greatest suffering (hell) would still await us all.

## Trekkies, Pay Attention

One of the most critically acclaimed Star Trek episodes of the entire series was the penultimate episode of the first season.[37] Titled "The City on the Edge of Forever," the episode involved the crew of the *USS Enterprise* discovering a portal which would transport them back in time. It revolves around the story of Edith Keeler, a peace advocate and noted social reformer, who had been killed when hit by a car. Dr. Leonard McCoy, using this portal, saves Keeler's life dramatically—and catastrophically alters history in the process. Keeler goes on to lead a pacifist movement that delays America's entry into World War II. This in turn allows the Nazis to develop the atomic bomb first, leading to world domination and millions more dying than would have had history not been changed.

To complicate matters, Captain Kirk, who has also traveled back to a time before McCoy's lifesaving event, falls in love with Edith Keeler. When he learns from Spock the consequences of what McCoy will do, Kirk is faced with either allowing Edith to die or allowing history to take this tragic turn. As he and Edith cross the street (she to the fated and fatal accident), Kirk holds McCoy back from saving her so that history remains on track and the world remains free from Nazi domination.[38]

The great (though I am sure unintended) spiritual lesson from this show is that, far from being pointless, what we may think are random senseless accidents may serve a greater purpose and effect a greater good. Such was the case at a place called Golgotha. God sees every possible outcome of every possible action, and the cross tells us that we can and must trust His hand to fit all evil and suffering into His glory and our good.[39]

## This Is a Test

One thing believers can always be certain of is that every trouble, trial, and tribulation that comes into our lives is always a test of our faith. Elisabeth Elliot said, "Every experience of trial puts us to this test: Do you trust God or don't you?"[40] Job said to his wife, who assailed God with bitterness over their misfortune, "Shall we accept good from God, and not trouble?"[41] It is easy to trust God in the good times, but that kind of trust is, in a sense, toothless. Faith with teeth in it clings to God with praise and tenacity regardless the circumstances.

The wisest man who ever lived wrote:" If you falter in a time of trouble, how small is your strength!"[42] Sometimes God allows troubles to come into our lives to show us just how strong, or how weak, our faith really is. God sometimes puts you in the kitchen of trouble just to see if your faith can take the heat.

Real faith is not always getting what you want from God. Real faith is accepting what you're given by God, and praising Him just the same. Take the problem of sickness. I believe in faith healing,[43] for all healing is divine healing. I have seen some miraculous healings in my ministry. But I cringe and almost gnash my teeth when I hear someone ask a sick person, "Do you have the faith to be healed?" I believe an even bigger question is, "Do you have the faith not to be healed and still praise and love God just the same?"

I have learned that it takes far more faith to endure trouble than it does to escape trouble. I heard someone say once, "The faith that cannot be tested cannot be trusted."

Job had the faith to say, "But he knows the way that I take; when he has tested me, I will come forth as gold."[44] The final stage of gold production—*refining*—removes impurities that remain after the smelting process.[45] God compares our faith to gold, where the impurities must be removed to produce the purest gold possible.

All that glitters is not gold. All that "believes" is not real faith. Real faith can stand the refining fire of suffering and undeserved evil and come out even stronger and more resilient. Real faith sees God as completely trustworthy. Real faith doesn't have to understand the "why" of everything that happens; it trusts in the "Who" over it. You never have to understand what God is doing if you know you can always trust God to do what is right. Remember, God never did give Job the one thing he asked for—an explanation for why "bad things happen to good people." What He wanted from Job, He wants from all of us—trust.

## The Best Is Yet to Be

I admit that one chapter on this difficult topic will not answer every question about why bad things happen. Entire tomes have attempted this and come up short. But I close with this thought: *For those of us who are Christians, every temporal evil and the suffering we experience in this life cannot compare to the eternal good and joy we will experience in the life to come.*

I didn't come up with that idea. The most prolific author of the New Testament, the greatest preacher/missionary/theologian who ever lived, who suffered everything from starvation to stoning, from mockery to martyrdom, from illness to imprisonment, wrote, "Our present sufferings are not worth comparing with the glory that will be revealed in us,"[46] and "Our light and momentary troubles are achieving for us an eternal glory that far outweighs them all."[47]

If a sovereign, compassionate, omniscient God resides in heaven, then we can rest assured that our temporary sufferings on earth will redound to our eternal benefit and our greatest good. If this is not so, we are resigned to injustice going unpunished and suffering having no purpose. We have already seen in the cross that if God had eliminated *that* greatest of all evil, He would have also eliminated the greatest of all good. The cross calls us to trust in a loving Father the same way His Son did when He willingly endured the greatest evil and suffering of all for the greatest good ever achieved.

Evil doesn't tell me that God doesn't exist or that if He does He isn't powerful. It tells me that God is so great that He can allow evil and suffering in this world and use it to accomplish an even greater good for us and, more to the point, for His eternal glory, which is the greatest good of all.

# Is Israel Still Special to You Today?

A few years ago I got from a young man an email that I took seriously. I immediately responded for a number of reasons. First, I knew him to be a bright student and avid reader. Second, he is a fine Christian young man with extremely high values. Third, he has a keen interest in both the Bible and the subject of the email. Fourth, I know his mom probably better than I know anybody in the world, and she is the greatest influence in my life. She expects me to always answer his calls or emails instantaneously, dropping everything I'm doing if necessary. Fifth, he's my son Jonathan.

Out of the blue, he sent this query: "Dear Dad: I am researching a theological question and need your help. Here is the question: How does the nation of Israel fit into the plan of God?"

It was a great question then and a great question now. You cannot understand the Middle Eastern political situation, much of Bible prophecy, or the present-day importance of the Arab-Israeli conflict if you don't understand the place of Israel in the plan of God. God's blueprint for the future is wrapped up in the Jewish people, and particularly the nation of Israel.

God early on assigned Israel a place of importance unparalleled by any other nation in history. For example, God made Israel the *geographical* center of the world. God Himself declared: "This is Jerusalem, which I have set in the center of the nations, with countries all around her."[1]

---

Jerusalem is the most important city in the biblical narrative and arguably all of history.

---

The ancient rabbis referred to Israel as "the navel of the earth." In the Church of the Holy Sepulcher in Jerusalem there is an inscription that reads: "This is the center of the earth." This tiny nation serves as the crossroads where Europe, Asia, and Africa all meet. Draw a circle with Jerusalem at its center and with a radius of just nine hundred miles, and that circle will include Athens, Istanbul, Antioch, Beirut, Damascus, Baghdad, Alexandria, Cairo, and Mecca. The history of Western Civilization is wrapped up in events that transpired in those ten cities, but none more important than what happened in Jerusalem.

Jerusalem is the most important city in the biblical narrative and arguably all of history. There has never been a city like it. This city is mentioned 804 times in Scripture, more than any other city. Both Israel and her capital hold unique geographical significance.

Furthermore, Israel is the *spiritual* center of the world. It was in Israel that Jesus was born, lived, and died. It's where His resurrection and ascension occurred, and it's where He will return. The three major religions of this world—Islam, Judaism, and Christianity—claim Jerusalem as a spiritual capital.

---

David exhorted, "Pray for the peace of Jerusalem."
Why did he not say, "Pray for peace on earth"?
Because peace will not come on earth
until it comes on Jerusalem.

---

Israel is the *prophetical* center of the world. If you want to know what time it is on God's clock, look at Israel. If you want to know what day it is on God's calendar, look at Israel. If you want to know what degree it is on God's thermometer, look at Israel. Any understanding of biblical eschatology must take the future fate of Israel into account.

It is the *political* center of the world. It is at Armageddon in northern Palestine that the last armies will fight the last battle of the last war. David exhorted, "Pray for the peace of Jerusalem."[2] Why did he not say, "Pray for peace on earth"? Because peace will not come on earth until it comes on Jerusalem, and there will be no peace in Jerusalem until the Prince of Peace returns.

Dr. Paige Patterson, president of Southwestern Baptist Theological Seminary in Fort Worth, Texas, recounts the story of meeting with Yasser Arafat, former head of the Palestine Liberation Organization, in the guesthouse of one of Saddam Hussein's palaces in Baghdad. They were discussing the possibilities of peace in the Middle East. Dr. Patterson proposed the one solution found in Scripture and read Arafat these words:

> In that day there will be a highway from Egypt to Assyria. The Assyrians will go to Egypt and the Egyptians to Assyria. The Egyptians and Assyrians will worship together. In that

day Israel will be the third, along with Egypt and Assyria, a blessing on the earth. The LORD Almighty will bless them, saying, "Blessed be Egypt my people, Assyria my handiwork, and Israel my inheritance."[3]

Patterson then said: "Mr. Arafat, there is coming a day when there will be peace in the Middle East, and in those days, God will say 'Assyria, My people; Egypt, My people; and Israel, My inheritance.' That peace can only come in the land and in the heart of an individual when Jesus is made the King."[4]

---

The only nation in history whose origin can be traced with total and complete accuracy is Israel.

---

Patterson was right. There will be no lasting peace in the world until there is peace in the Middle East. There will be no peace in the Middle East until there is peace in Jerusalem. There will be no peace in Jerusalem until Jesus returns. The key to political peace remains in possession of the fate of Israel.[5]

Israel as a nation is the crown jewel amongst all the countries and peoples God created. She holds a special place in God's heart and has since her founding. But why does she? How did she achieve this unique status?

## Back to the Future

The only nation in history whose origin can be traced with total and complete accuracy is Israel. No one knows who the first Englishman was. No one knows who the first Swede was. No one knows who the first German was. No one knows who the first Korean was. But the entire world knows the first Hebrew—Abraham.

The history of Israel begins with a literal miracle—a miraculous birth. The story unfolds with a nomadic couple named Abraham and Sarah. They were both so old that sexual intimacy for them consisted of holding hands and sighing wistfully. But then Dr. I Can Do Anything made a historic house call and said:

> "I will surely return to you about this time next year, and Sarah your wife will have a son."
>
> Now Sarah was listening at the entrance to the tent, which was behind him. Abraham and Sarah were already very old, and Sarah was past the age of childbearing. So Sarah laughed to herself as she thought, "After I am worn out and my lord is old, will I now have this pleasure?"
>
> Then the LORD said to Abraham, "Why did Sarah laugh and say, 'Will I really have a child, now that I am old?' Is anything too hard for the LORD? I will return to you at the appointed time next year, and Sarah will have a son."[6]

God had promised Abraham earlier that he would be the progenitor of a great and a mighty nation through which He would bless "all peoples on earth," a reference to the coming of Messiah.[7] Now He promised Abraham a son. When God promised Abraham this, he was the president of HARP—the Hebrew Association of Retired People. Abraham was nearly a hundred years old, and Sarah was no spring chicken at ninety. When God told them they would conceive a child, the last thing on either of their minds was Victoria's Secret.

Let's face it—you just don't find bestsellers titled "Sex and the *Very* Senior Adult." I am reminded of the ninety-five-year-old man who married a twenty-five-year old woman. When they got home from the wedding, the young bride looked at her old husband and tantalizingly said, "Would you like to go upstairs and spend some time with me?" He looked at her and said, "I can't do both."

All of the reproductive powers of Abraham and Sarah were dead. Millennia later, speaking of this event, Scripture records,

> Without weakening in his faith, [Abraham] faced the fact that his body was as good as dead—since he was about a hundred years old—and that Sarah's womb was also dead. Yet he did not waver through unbelief regarding the promise of God, but was strengthened in his faith and gave glory to God, being fully persuaded that God had power to do what he had promised.[8]

And God honored their faith, gave them a son, and a nation was born.

---

When God chose the nation of Israel, He gave her four things: a land, a law, a language, and a Lord.

---

Just as every Jewish person owes his or her origin to a miracle birth, every Christian owes his or her origin to a miracle birth—the virgin birth of our Lord Jesus Christ. So today thirteen million Jews (Hebrews) inhabit the earth, all because of the miraculous birth of a baby boy to a hundred-year-old father and a ninety-year-old mother who dared to believe God. No other nation in history has had such a miraculous beginning or such a promise of future blessing.

## The Future Is Now

No nation in history has a more fascinating story, which continues up to this moment, than does this tiny nation of only eight thousand square miles.[9] When God chose the nation of Israel, He gave her four things: a *land,* a *law,* a *language,* and a *Lord.* But Israel defiled the land, defied the law, deserted the language, and denied the Lord.

---

God made a promise to Israel that the day would come when she would be restored to the land and reclaim the land God had promised to her.

---

Israel turned away from the One who gave her the land, and God allowed the nation to be conquered and the people dispersed. God had given ample warning through Moses that this would happen, to no avail:

> However, if you do not obey the LORD your God and do not carefully follow all his commands and decrees I am giving you today, all these curses will come upon you and overtake you...
>
> The LORD will cause you to be defeated before your enemies. You will come at them from one direction but flee from them in seven, and you will become a thing of horror to all the kingdoms on earth...
>
> You will become a thing of horror, a byword and an object of ridicule among all the peoples where the LORD will drive you...
>
> Just as it pleased the LORD to make you prosper and increase in number, so it will please him to ruin and destroy you. You will be uprooted from the land you are entering to possess.
>
> Then the LORD will scatter you among all nations, from one end of the earth to the other. There you will worship other gods—gods of wood and stone, which neither you nor your ancestors have known.[10]

What God predicted is exactly what happened. Israel rebelled and rejected God, and the nation was overwhelmed by pagan nations and deported from the land. For thousands of years the Jews were dispersed, displaced, and despised by the nations. But God was not done with the Jewish people. His covenants still needed to be kept and prophecies fulfilled.

God made a promise to Israel that the day would come when she would be restored to the land and reclaim the land God had promised to her.[11] The prophet Jeremiah declared,

> "Hear the word of the LORD, you nations;
> proclaim it in distant coastlands:
> 'He who scattered Israel will gather them
> and will watch over his flock like a shepherd.'"[12]

The prophet Ezekiel was even more specific, predicting not just the return of the people but to a land better than they first found it:

> "Therefore say: 'This is what the Sovereign LORD says: I will gather you from the nations and bring you back from the countries where you have been scattered, and I will give you back the land of Israel again...'"

> "'But you, mountains of Israel, will produce branches and fruit for my people Israel, for they will soon come home. I am concerned for you and will look on you with favor; you will be plowed and sown, and I will cause many people to live on you—yes, all of Israel. The towns will be inhabited and the ruins rebuilt. I will increase the number of people and animals living on you, and they will be fruitful and become numerous. I will settle people on you as in the past and will make you PROSPER more than before. Then you will know that I am the LORD.'"[13]

These promises explain why the Jewish people can never be assimilated or eliminated. Today there are no Babylonians, no Hittites, no Philistines, and no Assyrians, but there are still Hebrews. This is not for a lack of trying on the part for her enemies through the centuries.

From around 1500 BC, when a new pharaoh came to the throne of Egypt and launched history's first attempt to exterminate the Jews by killing all firstborn Jewish males, to the relatively recent attempt by Adolf Hitler to provide "the final solution" via the Holocaust, to Islamic fanatics determined to destroy Israel once and for all, Israel has had a bull's-eye on her back unlike any other people in history. But the Jewish people are still here.

This resilience and seeming indestructibility moved Mark Twain to write:

> The Egyptian, the Babylonian, and the Persian rose, filled the planet with sound and splendor, then faded to dream-stuff and passed away; the Greek and the Roman followed, and made a vast noise and they are gone; other peoples have sprung up, held their torch high for a time, but it burned out and they sit in twilight now or have vanished.
>
> All things are mortal but the Jew; all other forces pass, but he remains. What is the secret of his immortality?[14]

For many biblical scholars, this phenomenon makes 1948 such a watershed year. After nearly two thousand years, a nation was born in a day; a nation that had been dormant and dead for two millennia came to life in one day in 1948. It is an incredible story that is truly inexplicable apart from the unique place of Israel in the mind of God and His plan for the world.

On May 14, 1948, the British Mandate over Palestine expired, and the Jewish People's Council gathered at the Tel Aviv Museum and approved a proclamation declaring the establishment of the State of Israel. The proclamation was read with an air of finality and almost defiance:

> On the 29th November, 1947, the United Nations General Assembly passed a resolution calling for the establishment

of a Jewish State in Eretz-Israel ["the land of Israel"]; the General Assembly required the inhabitants of Eretz-Israel to take such steps as were necessary on their part for the implementation of that resolution. This recognition by the United Nations of the right of the Jewish people to establish their State is irrevocable.

This right is the natural right of the Jewish people to be masters of their own fate, like all other nations, in their own sovereign State.

ACCORDINGLY WE, MEMBERS OF THE PEOPLE'S COUNCIL, REPRESENTATIVES OF THE JEWISH COMMUNITY OF ERETZ-ISRAEL AND OF THE ZIONIST MOVEMENT, ARE HERE ASSEMBLED ON THE DAY OF THE TERMINATION OF THE BRITISH MANDATE OVER ERETZ-ISRAEL AND, BY VIRTUE OF OUR NATURAL AND HISTORIC RIGHT AND ON THE STRENGTH OF THE RESOLUTION OF THE UNITED NATIONS GENERAL ASSEMBLY, HEREBY DECLARE THE ESTABLISHMENT OF A JEWISH STATE IN ERETZ-ISRAEL, TO BE KNOWN AS THE STATE OF ISRAEL.[15]

At that moment approximately 650,000 Jewish people lived in the land. Forty million Arabs, who immediately declared war and vowed to drive them into the sea, surrounded them. That tiny nation was outnumbered in soldiers, out-equipped in arms, outclassed in vehicles. They were outnumbered 40 to 1 in troops; 100 to 1 in population; 1000 to 1 in military equipment.[16]

Just twenty-four hours before the United Nations recognized Israel, a Jewish person could be arrested for even carrying a gun. In one day the nation had to defend herself against six Arab states. But miraculously, she won that war and two more wars after that.[17] Today with a population of only 7.5 million people, Israel is the fourth strongest military power in the world, and the only Middle Eastern nation that produces its own tanks, planes, and weapons.

## Changes in Israel Since 1948

Just what has happened since Israel was reborn? First, as God predicted, *the land has been revived.*

> "I will bring my people Israel back from exile.
> They will rebuild the ruined cities and live in them.
>    They will plant vineyards and drink their wine;
>       they will make gardens and eat their fruit.
> I will plant Israel in their own land,
>    never again to be uprooted
>    from the land I have given them,"
>          says the LORD your God.[18]

You wouldn't know it now, but the Israel of sixty years ago was a wasteland filled with rocks and dirt; 60 percent of the land was barren desert. But no more. Even though it rains only in the winter and water is scarce, the land now blossoms like a rose because of the most effective irrigation system in the world. Today, Israel is one of a handful of nations that produces enough food to feed itself and to feed others.

Just sixty years ago the beautiful Valley of Armageddon was a mosquito-infested swamp. But now it is a fertile valley that yields four different crops a year. In the last thirty-five years, over 100 million trees have been planted on barren hills and desert soil.

*The law has been reinstituted.* Even though God-fearing Orthodox Jews make up only 5 percent of the population of Israel, the foundational cornerstone of the law—the Sabbath—has been established. It is the law of the land for everyone in Israel, from sunup to sundown. On the Sabbath, restaurants are closed, buses do not run, there is no television, and except for emergencies, even hospitals shut down.[19]

*The Hebrew language has been resurrected.* It is common knowledge that almost the entire Old Testament was written in Hebrew.[20] Yet Hebrew as a spoken language may have already fallen out of everyday use even in the time of the Lord Jesus Christ. Until the twentieth century, no one had spoken the language for a couple thousand years. Then a man named Eliezer Ben Yehuda had a vision to revive the Hebrew language. He took a vow never to speak any other language, and began to teach his children to speak in Hebrew. On September 23, 1922, the League of Nations officially recognized Hebrew as a spoken language of the world. It is the only major dead language that has been restored to life in the history of mankind.[21]

When the Roman Empire ruled the world, Latin was the universal language. Who speaks Latin today as a primary language? No one to my knowledge, and perhaps the following anecdote tells why. A high school student struggling with Latin wrote this on a bathroom wall:

> Latin is a dead language
> As dead as dead can be;
> It killed the Roman Empire,
> And now it's killing me.

Latin was a major language in its day but no more. But in Israel today, Hebrew is the native and the mother tongue.

*Jewish people have made significant contributions to the world.* Jews made up 10 percent of the population of the Roman Empire. If they were the same proportion of the world's population today, they would number 200 million people; but there are only 13 million Jewish people in the world. Only one-quarter of 1 percent of the world's population is Jewish. They are not many, but they are mighty. They have won a far disproportionate share of all the honors in medicine, health, music, public life, and science, including an amazing 20 percent of all

Nobel Prizes given to date.[22] Most of us have no idea how much daily life is affected every day by the Jewish people.

- Have you ever taken an aspirin for a headache? Friedrich Bayer, who developed the aspirin, was Jewish.

- Have you ever been vaccinated for polio? Jonas Salk, who developed this vaccine, was Jewish.

- Have you ever had a doctor prescribe the antibiotic streptomycin? Selman Waksman, who developed that antibiotic, was a Jew.

- Do you take vitamins? The man who developed and discovered vitamins was a Jewish man named Casimir Funk.

- Have you or a loved one ever had to take chemotherapy. The man who discovered and developed the medical treatment of chemotherapy was Paul Ehrlich, who is Jewish.

- If you have ever been tested for venereal disease, which we all were before we got married, you were given the Wassermann test. August von Wassermann was Jewish.

- The most prestigious association of doctors in the world is the American Medical Association. It was founded by Isaac Hays, who is Jewish.

- Perhaps the most famous scientist who ever lived, who discovered the Theory of Relativity, was Albert Einstein, who was Jewish.

- The founder of psychoanalysis, the precursor of much modern day psychiatry was Sigmund Freud, a Jew.

---

Israel is a divinely chosen people. God promised
their founder that they would be a blessing to
the entire world—a promise not made to
any other nation in history.

---

I don't believe this phenomenon is a coincidence; I believe it is providence. Israel is a divinely chosen people. God promised their founder that they would be a blessing to the entire world—a promise not made to any other nation in history.[23]

Looking down the corridor of history to the present, what do we see? One foreign policy analyst summarized Israel's journey succinctly:

> A powerless people, scattered around the globe, victims of perhaps the greatest catastrophe in human history, are granted international legitimacy to create a state of their own in their ancient homeland.
>
> A poorly trained, poorly equipped Jewish army defeats the combined might of the Arab world. Later, a better trained, better equipped army defeats not once but three times, Arab forces with greater arsenals and manpower. And now, a nation the size of New Jersey boasts one of the most powerful armies in the world.
>
> A nation of immigrants from more than 100 countries, including those with authoritarian governments, becomes a democracy that is so vibrant and pluralistic that it is criticized for having too many political parties in the government.
>
> In less than 60 years, the Jewish population of Israel has grown by a factor of twelve, from half a million to more than six million.
>
> In those six decades, a land of deserts and malarial swamps is built by blood, sweat, and tears into one of the most technologically advanced countries on the globe, a place where America's premier high-tech companies set up research and development facilities.
>
> Universities in Israel become world class, as does its premier hospital, Hadassah.
>
> The ancient Jewish community of Ethiopia is transported on the wings of eagles to the Promised Land.

The long-suffering Jews of the Soviet Union witness the collapse of Communism and more than one million immigrate to Israel.

Israel signs peace treaties with Egypt and Jordan.

Israel has one of the highest economic growth rates in the world.

The most powerful nation on earth develops a special relationship with the Jewish state.[24]

I admit I write as a pastor and a theologian, not a historian. From my perspective, Israel's existence is the proverbial "God-thing," and I believe it is the one truly invincible nation on earth. If that sounds like the mother of all overstatements, ponder this scriptural reminder:

> This is what the LORD says,
> he who appoints the sun
>    to shine by day,
> who decrees the moon and the stars
>    to shine by night,
> who stirs up the sea
>    so that its waves roar—
>    the LORD Almighty is his name:
> "Only if these decrees vanish from my sight,"
>    declares the LORD,
> "will Israel ever cease
>    being a nation before me."[25]

What an incredible promise. Only if the sun stops rising, the moon quits shining, and the waves of the sea cease crashing on shore will Israel cease to exist. China, the United States, Russia all could cease to exist...but not this nation.[26]

My good friend Bryant Wright, currently president of the Southern Baptist Convention, answers the question about Israel straightforwardly:

The questioning [concerning the roots of the Middle East conflict] usually begins with "Does God play favorites?" In light of all the biblical teaching we have looked at, the answer is obvious. Absolutely yes! Out of all the people in history, God chose Abraham...Isaac over Ishmael...Jacob over Esau to be his heir to the covenant commitment to Abraham. God chose Israel over Egypt, Assyria, Babylon, Persia, Greece, Rome, America and all the other kingdoms of the earth to be His specially chosen people.[27]

*The Lord is still rejected.* But Israel still has one glaring shortcoming. Even though she is in the land, following some semblance of the law, once again speaking the language, she continues to turn her back on God. Though considered a religious nation, less than 20 percent of the people living in the land practice the Jewish faith. As many as 70 percent have no religious beliefs, and as few as 10 percent can realistically be called "observant Jews" who actually attend synagogue.[28]

## It Ain't Over Till It's Over

God's purpose for Israel far transcends her home—His greater desire is for her heart. Land is not nearly as important to Him as Lordship. He wants His people to surrender to the greatest Jew of all, Jesus Christ. He wants this nation who once rejected Him to receive Him; who once crucified Him to crown Him; who once cried out against Him to cry out for Him. God Himself has guaranteed that day is going to come.

> "The days are coming," declares the LORD,
>     "when I will make a new covenant
> with the people of Israel
>     and with the people of Judah.
> It will not be like the covenant
>     I made with their ancestors

> when I took them by the hand
>    to lead them out of Egypt,
> because they broke my covenant,
>    though I was a husband to them,"
>    declares the LORD.
> "This is the covenant I will make with the
>    people of Israel
>    after that time," declares the LORD.
> "I will put my law in their minds
>    and write it on their hearts.
> I will be their God
>    and they will be my people.
> No longer will they teach their neighbor,
>    or say to one another, 'Know the LORD,'
> because they will all know me,
>    from the least of them to the greatest,"
>    declares the LORD.
> "For I will forgive their wickedness
>    and will remember their sins no more."[29]

Paul even declares unequivocally that the day is coming when "all Israel will be saved."[30] Yet when less than 1 percent of all Jewish people in the world are followers of Jesus Christ and accept him as the Messiah, the question begs to be asked, How is this going to happen?

It is not difficult to notice that most world opinion is hardened against the nation of Israel. This antipathy toward Israel will increase as the last days approach. Yet even that is for a divine reason. God, speaking through the prophet Zechariah, proclaimed many centuries ago, "On that day, when all the nations of the earth are gathered against her, I will make Jerusalem an immovable rock for all the nations. All who try to move it will injure themselves."[31]

All the nations of the world are eventually going to try to finish the "final solution" that Hitler envisioned. Every nation on earth will join forces to destroy Israel once and for all. It will look as if the final curtain has been drawn on the act called Israel, the nation that seemingly refused to die.

But at the exact moment when it appears all is lost and that the antichrist, along with the entire world, will finally finish the job of destroying this special people, the Lord Jesus is going to come to the rescue:

> I will gather all the nations to Jerusalem to fight against it; the city will be captured, the houses ransacked, and the women raped. Half of the city will go into exile, but the rest of the people will not be taken from the city. Then the LORD will go out and fight against those nations, as he fights in a day of battle.[32]

Just as it appears all is lost and the "good ship Israel" is going down for good, in a flash the tide will turn. Just like the cavalry in the old cowboy movies, the Lord Jesus is going to come at the last minute and deliver Israel from certain destruction. When that happens this will be Israel's response:

> "And I will pour out on the house of David and the inhabitants of Jerusalem a spirit of grace and supplication. They will look on me, the one they have pierced, and they will mourn for him as one mourns for an only child, and grieve bitterly for him as one grieves for a firstborn son."[33]

Scales of blindness will finally fall from Israel's eyes. Her heart will be softened, and in an instant, an entire nation that for two millennia and counting has said a vociferous *No* to Christ will say an everlasting *Yes* to her true Messiah. Then the true impact of the following passage will be finally understood and appreciated:

"How great you are, Sovereign LORD! There is no one like you, and there is no God but you, as we have heard with our own ears. And who is like your people Israel—the one nation on earth that God went out to redeem as a people for himself, and to make a name for himself, and to perform great and awesome wonders by driving out nations and their gods from before your people, whom you redeemed from Egypt? *You have established your people Israel as your very own forever,* and you, LORD, have become their God."[34]

When God says something, He says what He means and He means what He says. Israel is the only nation in history of the world that has this divine promise. God still has a plan, a purpose, and a promise for Israel. All of history is moving toward the keeping of that promise and the fulfillment of that plan and purpose.

---

This nation stands as a daily reminder that
God is faithful even when we are not.

---

The nation of Israel teaches us three truths about God we should never forget:

- God's people cannot be destroyed.
- God's promise cannot be denied.
- God's purpose cannot be defeated.

Israel *is* special. But so are all who call upon the name of the Lord. This nation stands as a daily reminder that God is faithful even when we are not.[35] It is the "Holy Land" only because of the favor it enjoys from a Holy Lord. That is a truth that neither we nor Israel should ever forget.

CHAPTER SIX

# I Thought You Were Loving...
# Will You Really Send
# People to Hell?

I still remember the first time she came to our home. My middle son
met her during his senior year in high school, and they immediately
became fast friends. She was the perky sort: short, lithe, jet-black hair,
piercing eyes, and a smile that could light up the darkest room.

Kim was born in Japan and her family lives outside of Tokyo,
though she moved here when she was thirteen. She has adapted to
life in America well and is as westernized as any native-born American
young lady. But one palpable difference far transcended her Japanese
heritage. Jonathan was so sensitive to this difference and was so ada-
mant that I share this sensitivity that the tension is within me to this
day whenever Kim visits.

If you were in our home during her stay, you would notice nothing unusual. We love Kim and get along with her great. She is kind, gracious, and humble in keeping with her Japanese culture and upbringing. She is fun to be with and a joy to be around.

Kim is aware that our family is Christian. When we eat, we pray in the name of Jesus, and she takes no offense. She shows great respect to us in every way and blesses our home with her presence. So why the tension?

The problem in a nutshell is hell. Kim comes from a Buddhist background. Her extended family is Buddhist as is her immediate family, though they are not devout. Yet, therein lies the problem for Kim.

As Jonathan has gently tried to share Christ with her, she always asks him this question: "If Jesus is the only way to heaven, as you say, then that means my ancestors resting in the family tomb back in Japan are in hell now. How do you expect me to accept that? How could your loving God send anyone to hell?"

Every time Kim enters our home, I think of her question with both anguish and yet firm conviction that hell is real and must really be dealt with.

Hell is a topic that frequently generates considerable controversy. A few years ago, hell was front-page news. After Scott Peterson was found guilty of murdering his wife, Laci, Laci's mother, Sharon Rocha, spoke these words and more directly to him in the sentencing phase of his trial:

> Now it is time for you to take responsibility for murdering Laci and Conner, your son, your own flesh and blood... You want to know what your son was thinking while you murdered him? He said, "Daddy, please don't kill us. Mommy has enough love for both of us. I promise I won't take her away from you. Daddy, why are you killing us?

Please, please stop." And now, Scott Peterson, I'm saying this to you: "You deserve to burn in hell for all eternity."[1]

Mrs. Rocha's last statement raises some huge questions. Is there a hell? The predominant twenty-first century worldview is that hell is at worst a state of mind and at best a place most people don't have to worry about. Does anybody really deserve to go there—forever? Even those who may concede that it is a real place believe that few people (if any) deserve to go there for all eternity.

For example, many more Americans believe in heaven than believe in hell. For every American who believes they are hell-bound, 120 believe they are heaven-bound.[2] As Mark Driscoll pithily puts it, "Apparently Hell is for the other guy—the terrorist, the relief pitcher that gives up a lot of walks, and anyone who wears a suit and works in Washington DC."[3]

John Lennon, the former Beatle, had a smash hit in the early 1970s with a song that included the words "imagine there's no heaven" and "no hell below us."[4]

Lennon expressed perfectly and poetically the popular sentiment of many—there is no hell. Hell is the figment of some "hellfire and damnation" fundamentalist preacher who sweats profusely, slings spit, and screams at the top of his lungs, "Turn or burn!"

For others, if hell exists, it's just "the hell we create on earth."

A young lady went to her mother crying, and her mother said, "What's wrong?"

She said, "Mother, I can't marry John. He has a religion that believes hell doesn't exist."

"Go ahead and marry him," her mother said. "He'll find out."

Yet, what's so strange is that even though in our culture the reality and concept of hell is either dead or in intensive care, the word *hell* has never been more popular or commonly used. One newspaper colum-nist even asked why our society is so schizophrenic about hell. How is it that *hell* is one of the most commonly used words in the English lan-guage, yet one of the least talked about?[5] Consider:

- A reckless driver is described as "hell on wheels."
- When we witness extreme violence or a major argument we say, "All hell broke loose."
- We say that a bad spouse is "hell to live with."
- A great effort means you are "trying like hell."
- If someone is really pumped up about something, they will say, "I'm as excited as hell."
- If you want to move quickly, you go like "a bat out of hell."
- The odds of winning the lottery? "A snowball's chance in hell."
- What does the troublemaker do? "Raise hell."
- You threaten someone by saying, "There will be hell to pay."
- If something is painful, "it hurts like hell."
- Before some people will vote for a particular political party, "hell will freeze over."

So the question is, "Is hell more than just a figure of speech, a joke, or an antiquated fear-mongering myth?" The question of hell is a hel-lacious question, and the following questions deserve honest answers from God's Word:

- Is there a place called hell?
- Do people really go to hell? If so, who and why?
- How could a loving God send anyone to hell?

As I deal with this question, which has been asked of me multiple times by both believer and nonbeliever, I share the sentiment of C.S. Lewis who said, "There is no doctrine which I would more willingly remove from Christianity than [hell], if it lay in my power...I would pay any price to be able to say truthfully: 'All will be saved.'"[6]

So would I. But one cannot remain loyal to either the Son of God or the Word of God and jettison hell. Truth is tough, and no truth tougher to frame and face than hell; but the truth must be told.

## Jesus on Hell

If you were to ask any reputable theologian, preacher, or religious scholar to name the greatest sermon ever preached, that might appear at first glance to be an impossible question to answer and would probably ignite a fierce debate. (Frankly, most of us pastors probably think our messages are greater than they really are.) But this question not surprisingly gets an almost unanimous answer: The Sermon on the Mount is hands down the greatest sermon ever preached. To quote just one man, former president Franklin Roosevelt said: "I doubt if there is in the world a single problem, whether social, political, or economic, which would not find ready solution if men and nations would rule their lives according to the plain teaching of the Sermon on the Mount."[7]

---

Surprising though it may be, Jesus spoke more about hell than any other person in the Bible.

---

I cannot help but wonder how much President Roosevelt had read this Scripture, because Jesus had not gotten far into the Sermon on the Mount when He makes these statements:

> "But I say to you that everyone who is angry with his brother
> shall be guilty before the court; and whoever says to his

brother, 'You good-for-nothing,' shall be guilty before the supreme court; and whoever says, 'You fool,' shall be guilty enough to go into the *fiery hell*...

"But I say to you that everyone who looks at a woman with lust for her has already committed adultery with her in his heart. If your right eye makes you stumble, tear it out and throw it from you; for it is better for you to lose one of the parts of your body, than for your whole body to be thrown into *hell*. If your right hand makes you stumble, cut it off and throw it from you; for it is better for you to lose one of the parts of your body, than for your whole body to go into *hell*."[8]

---

Of the 1,870 verses in the New Testament that record the words of Jesus, 13 percent deal with hell and judgment.

---

These words are not unusual coming from the lips of Jesus. Surprising though it may be, Jesus spoke more about hell than any other person in the Bible. For some it is not just surprising—it is both disappointing and disillusioning. The famous atheist Bertrand Russell stated: "There is one very serious defect to my mind in Christ's moral character, and that is that he believed in Hell. I do not myself feel that any person who is profoundly humane can believe in everlasting punishment."[9] Apart from the oddity of an atheist passing judgment on the most humane person who ever lived, is the question of who to believe—Russell or Jesus?

A theologian even weighs in with a scathing indictment of Christians who believe in hell: I consider the concept of hell as endless torment in body and mind an outrageous doctrine…How can Christians possibly project a deity of such cruelty and vindictiveness whose ways include inflicting everlasting torture upon his creatures, *however sinful they may have been?* Surely a God who would do such a thing is more nearly like Satan than like God.[10]

Like Russell, this theologian is indicting Jesus indirectly as He is the leading proponent of hell in the entire Bible.

Of the 1,870 verses in the New Testament that record the words of Jesus, 13 percent deal with hell and judgment. Jesus talked more about hell than any other topic. Of the forty parables Jesus told, more than half relate to hell and God's eternal judgment. The strongest biblical word for hell, the word *Gehenna,* is used twelve times in the Greek New Testament, and eleven times Jesus was the speaker.[11]

*WARNING: graphic depiction of hell to follow.*

The picture Jesus Christ painted of this place is not pretty. *Gehenna* refers to the Valley of Hinnom, which was located just south of Jerusalem. I have seen it, and it is a desolate, barren field to this day. In Jesus' day, it was used as a garbage dump where both trash and the bodies of executed criminals were burned. It was the most repugnant place in the entire city.

Jesus compared this place to hell because hell is a place of unspeakable, incomparable anguish and sorrow. It is a place of *emotional anguish*. Jesus, speaking of the future of those who reject God, said: "The Son of Man will send his angels, and they will gather out of his kingdom all causes of sin and all law-breakers, and throw them into the fiery furnace. In that place there will be weeping and gnashing of teeth."[12]

Why are the people there gnashing their teeth? Part of the emotional anguish of hell's inhabitants will be expressed by this continual, never-ending gnashing of the teeth, when people realize, "I blew it! Hell is real after all. Why did I ignore God and His mercy?"

Jesus also said that hell was a place of *physical pain*. In the verse just quoted, Jesus referred to hell as a "fiery furnace." Another description of hell states: "And the devil who deceived them was thrown into the lake of fire and brimstone, where the beast and the false prophet are also; and they will be tormented day and night forever and ever."[13]

Whatever else this verse means, hell is going to be a place of terrible pain.

At this point a question always arises: "Do you really believe it is a literal lake of fire? Do you really believe it is a fiery furnace? Do you really buy all that fire and brimstone stuff?" Whether it is literal or metaphorical, whether the fire and the furnace are real or not, the pain is real, the suffering is real, and the agony is real.[14]

---

Hell is the only hopeless place in the universe. In this life we can always say, "We'll get you next time," or "There's always tomorrow." In hell, there is no next time, no tomorrow; it is eternal.

---

Furthermore, Jesus also said it is a place of *relational isolation*: "And cast the worthless servant into the outer darkness. In that place there will be weeping and gnashing of teeth."[15] Darkness is a metaphor for loneliness and complete isolation. Mark Twain famously said, "I will take Heaven for climate, Hell for company." Twain, I am afraid, has been greatly disappointed.

In hell, you won't find fellowship, or relationship. In essence, hell is the place of eternal solitary confinement.

Jesus also said hell was a place of *eternal punishment*: "And these will go away into eternal punishment, but the righteous into eternal life."[16]

Hell is the only hopeless place in the universe. In this life we can always say, "We'll get you next time," or "There's always tomorrow," or

"Wait till next year." In hell, there is no next time, no tomorrow, no next year; it is eternal.

Again, these are the words of Jesus. Here is the choice. If hell is a myth or what Jesus said about hell is not true, then Jesus Christ lied and was neither a great teacher nor a good man, and He is certainly not the Son of God. To deny hell is to deny both the veracity and therefore the deity of Jesus.

## God and Hell

I have found that the single biggest rebuttal of hell that others make is the dogmatic statement: "A loving God would never send people to hell." I completely agree with that statement as is. However, three words in that statement make it completely misleading.

The first word is *loving*. God is a loving God, but His love is not just a sentimental emotion, some warm, fuzzy feeling that is tolerant of everything and everybody. God is a loving God, but His love is a holy love, a righteous love, and a just love.

---

God wants everyone to choose to love Him and be a part of His family, but *He will not force anyone to do so.*

---

It is true that God is so loving He has no desire for anyone to go to hell. Speaking through Ezekiel the prophet, He says, "As surely as I live, says the Sovereign LORD, I take no pleasure in the death of wicked people. I only want them to turn from their wicked ways so they can live."[17] God's heart toward the human race is affirmed just as clearly by the apostle Peter: "The Lord is not slow in keeping his promise, as some understand slowness. Instead he is patient with you, not wanting anyone to perish, but everyone to come to repentance."[18]

The Bible is clear. God hates hell and He hates people going there.

But God's love also requires that people be allowed to choose hell if that is what they want. This aspect of God's relationship to the human race is crucial to understand.

God wants everyone to choose to love Him and be a part of His family, but *He will not force anyone to do so*. We cannot have it both ways. Either we are robots, pawns in God's predetermined chess game, or we are creatures with the freedom to choose. It is the concept of choice that demands there must be a hell. As Hank Hanegraaff puts it:

> Without hell, none have a choice. And without choice, heaven would not be heaven; heaven would be hell. The righteous would inherit a counterfeit heaven, and the unrighteous would be incarcerated in heaven against their wills, which would be a torture worse than hell.[19]

Heaven and hell should not be seen as surprise outcomes or as being foisted on anyone apart from their personal preference. Both destinies are the logical final destination resulting from how one lived and operated on earth. Just as heaven is the joyful anticipation of one who *wants* to spend eternity with God, hell for the unbeliever is "a final divorce from God,"[20] the God he wanted no part of on earth.

Consider the atheist. How could one who so despised the concept of a sovereign God be at all happy consigned to spending eternity in His presence. Truly it is not so much God who rejects the atheist as the atheist who rejects God. God simply grants the atheist his wish to be away from Him forever.[21] C.S. Lewis said it best: "No one ever goes to hell deservingly—and no one ever goes to hell unwillingly."[22]

This world is filled with people who reject God's love every day, who have no desire to worship God's Son, who have no hunger to hear God's Word or fellowship with God's people. They would be miserable in heaven where these activities go on for eternity.

Imagine someone who has no time for God, no desire for God, no hunger for God, who hates the thought of going to a church and sitting through a worship service. Now imagine that person ending up in heaven in an eternal church service where twelve o'clock never comes, spending eternity with people who love God, praise God, and worship the God they never knew and never cared for? You can understand that person saying "hell no" to heaven.

God's love in a true sense demands a hell for those who don't want His love. Think about a man proposing to a woman and asking her to marry him. The woman says, "I respect you. I admire you. But I don't love you and I don't want to marry you." Imagine that he proposes to her a second time and she declines, and a third time and she declines. Finally, the man says, "You know what? I love you so much I'm going to force you to marry me. I'm going to force you to spend your life with me." Would you agree that really wouldn't be love? God's love is so great He is never going to force people to choose Him or go to a heaven they want no part of.

> Hell is not a sentence that God passes on sinners who reject Him. It is the end of a path that is freely chosen in this life day by day.

Choice also takes care of the second key word in the dogmatic statement, "A loving God would never *send* people to hell." God doesn't *send* anyone to hell. He gives people what they choose. If you believe that a human being has the right to choose and the ability to choose, then that demands that you believe in hell. If choice is limited only to loving God and going to heaven, then no real choice exists. Philosopher and theologian Norman Geisler said that the alternative to hell is worse than hell itself, because it would rob human beings of freedom and dignity by forcing them to go to a heaven they didn't want to go to in the first place and robbing them of their free choice.[23]

Hell is not a sentence that God passes on sinners who reject Him. It is the end of a path that is freely chosen in this life (here and now) day by day. To every person on earth who kept God at arm's length, who said by their actions and their thoughts, "We don't want any part of You, Your Son, Your salvation, Your grace, or Your worship, You keep Your distance and we will keep ours," God says, "You want distance? I will give you what you want—the ultimate distance. I will give you an eternity totally separated from Me."

The real question is this: *Why would a loving God force sinners to go to heaven?* Hell is giving what a person has said all his life that he wants—No God—because in hell that is exactly what you have—No God. It is the eternal fruit of an earthly life that was lived totally apart from God.

The third key word in the statement, "A loving God would never send people to hell," is *people.* That sounds so innocent, but it's not simply "people" who go to hell. Only sinners who refuse to admit they are sinners, repent and turn away from their sins, and receive God's forgiveness through Jesus Christ go to hell.

But just what is the sin that really deserves hell? The answer, which gets to the crux of why unrepentant, unforgiven sinners go to hell, may stun you.

According to the Bible, the most horribly sinful thing a person can ever do is not murder, rape, homosexuality, child molestation, fornication, treason, or incest. All these vices are horrible, but they cannot compare to the mocking, dishonoring, and rejecting of the supreme love of a God who went to such great lengths to save us that He sent His own Son to die for our sins.

Lest you think I am overstating the case, listen to this description of what a person is really doing when they fail to respond to God's gracious offer of salvation:

> Just think how much worse the punishment will be for those who have trampled on the Son of God, and have treated the blood of the covenant, which made us holy, as if it were common and unholy, and have insulted and disdained the Holy Spirit who brings God's mercy to us.[24]

The Greek word for "trampled" was used to describe salt that was considered worthless, having lost its flavor, and was thrown on the roads to be trampled underfoot. In essence, the person who rejects God's Son and God's grace is saying that His death and the blood He shed on the cross is absolutely worthless and meaningless. It is the attitude of a Ted Turner, who once said, "I don't want anybody to die for me. I've had a few drinks and a few girlfriends, and if that's gonna put me in hell, well, then so be it."[25]

---

If somehow everybody is going to wind up in heaven anyway, why the cross of Jesus Christ?

---

Also, don't get the idea that if people in hell had a second chance, they would do the right thing about Jesus Christ. C.S. Lewis said, "I willingly believe the damned are in one sense successful rebels to the end; that the doors of hell are locked on the inside."[26] Even in hell people would not choose to go to heaven, because in order to do that, they would have to do the one thing they definitely did not want to do on earth, which is surrender their lives to the God they denied.

## The Good News About Hell

We must remember that God never prepared hell for you and me. Jesus made a statement about hell that clues us in on why hell was created to begin with: "Then he will say to those on his left, 'Depart from me, you who are cursed, into the eternal fire prepared for the devil and his angels.'"[27]

Hell was designed for the devil and his angels, not for human beings. God sent His Son to die on a cross, thus providing a way for humans to avoid hell entirely. It's the bad news of hell that makes the good news of heaven so wonderful. "To play down hell and other harsh doctrines of the Christian faith does irreparable damage to our deepest comforts—our understanding of God's grace and love and of our human dignity and value to him. To preach the good news, we must [also] preach the bad."[28]

In fact the cross of Christ raises a huge question about hell: *If there is no hell or if somehow everybody is going to wind up in heaven anyway, why the cross of Jesus Christ?* To the question, "How could a loving God send people to hell?" I pose a greater question: *How could a loving God send His Son to die on the cross when He didn't have to?* Nothing short of the reality of hell can explain the cross of Jesus Christ.

Furthermore, the cross clarifies one last misconception about hell and who goes there. Most people who do believe in hell believe basically two things about who is going there and who isn't: *Good people go to heaven; bad people go to hell.*

At first blush that sounds fair. It sounds simple. It sounds like a good idea. The only problem is, it isn't true.

Do you know why? If good people went to heaven, heaven would be an empty place because the Bible says there aren't any good people. Compared to a perfectly holy God, no one qualifies as good, much less perfect. Solomon wrote,

> Indeed, there is no one on earth who is righteous,
> no one who does what is right and never sins.[29]

The Bible says you cannot be so good that you deserve to go to heaven nor so bad you have to go to hell. There are only two types of people on this planet: sinners who think they are saints, and saints who know they are sinners.[30]

Two men were sitting in a restaurant. One man got angry at the other and said to him, "Go to hell." A Christian reading his Bible happened to be sitting in the next booth, and he turned around and tapped this man on the shoulder and said, "I've been reading the directions, and you don't have to go if you don't want to."

That is the message of the Bible. You don't have to go if you don't want to. If you are an *unbeliever*, hell is real. But God didn't create hell for you, and you can go to heaven if you will receive Jesus Christ and His forgiveness. If you are a *believer*, you ought to live every day rejoicing in your salvation, thankful that you are going to heaven, and grateful to God that His grace has found you.

The greatest evangelist in history was speaking at a university in Wellington on New Zealand's North Island. He spoke about, among other things, the reality of hell. After the meeting, shortly before midnight, there was a loud knock on his door. He opened it to face an angry student.

"What do you mean coming over here from America and talking about hell? I don't believe in hell, and you have no right to come over here and talk about it!"

Billy Graham responded, "Let me ask you a question. Suppose you went to Auckland to catch a plane for Sydney. And suppose they told you there was a ten percent chance the plane wouldn't make it. Would you get on?"

"No, I wouldn't," the student replied.

"Well, what if there were only a five percent chance the plane wasn't going to make it? Would you get on then?"

"No, of course not."

"Now suppose there's only a ten percent chance—or even just a five percent chance—that Jesus was right and there *is* a hell. Do you think there's at least a five percent chance that He might have been right?"

"Well, yes, I suppose there is."

"Then is it worth taking the risk and ignoring those odds?"

"No. No it isn't."

"Then will you receive Christ and begin to follow Him?"

"No, I can't because I find that's not my problem. My real problem is that I don't want to live up to the standard that Jesus demands."[31]

That young student perfectly illustrates why so many have a problem with hell. It is not an intellectual problem. It is a spiritual and volitional problem. Jesus told the truth about hell and did us all a favor when He did. How we respond is up to us. Choose wisely, my friend.

CHAPTER SEVEN

# If You Care for and Love Gay People, Why Should I Care About Homosexuality?

His name is Vaughn Walker. Unless you are a lawyer in California or a federal judge, chances are you've never heard of him. But on August 4, 2010, he suddenly became more famous than Perry Mason.

Before that date Walker's only claim to fame was his position as chief judge of the United States District Court for the Northern District of California. But everything changed with a decision he rendered in *Perry v. Schwarzenegger*. It is one of the most breathtaking decisions ever rendered in American judicial history.[1]

The case revolved around the now famous Proposition 8 passed by California voters in November 2008, in which the majority endorsed a constitutional amendment that reads, "Only marriage between a man and a woman is valid or recognized in California." With the simple stroke of his judicial pen, Judge Walker declared unconstitutional every argument put forth by those defending the definition of marriage that has been the universal norm throughout every civilization from time immemorial.[2] California voters were told in no uncertain terms that they had no right to keep the traditional definition of marriage and that thousands of years of wisdom and consensus were null and void.

The central thrust of Walker's decision was to normalize homosexuality and deny the moral superiority of heterosexual relations within marriage over homosexual relations.[3] Walker dogmatically states, "Same-sex couples are identical to opposite-sex couples in the characteristics relevant to the ability to form successful marital unions."[4] He then lowers this legal boom: "Gender no longer forms an essential part of marriage; marriage under law is a union of equals."[5]

So what is a Christian who takes the Bible seriously to do when Scripture records unequivocally, as I will demonstrate in this chapter, a verdict on homosexuality and all sex outside of marriage diametrically opposed to the opinions of Judge Walker and an increasing percentage of American society? This poses no small problem for the Christian faith.[6]

Today many young people and adults rebel against Christianity because of its teaching on such things as premarital sex, homosexuality, adultery, and lust. In some ways, there may not be a more "no-win" topic to address than this one.

My friend Bill from Wisconsin, a former practicing homosexual who has come out of the gay lifestyle, emailed me the following after he saw a television broadcast of a message I preached on homosexuality:

> Dear Pastor Merritt:
> Thanks very much for your "H" bomb sermon. I am a gay man that decided not to turn you off that day and I learned so much from your message. My sexual preference will always

be gay. On the other hand, *we must follow God's laws about sexual conduct.* I was surprised that many gays believe in living a chaste and celibate life. Not all gays are for same sex marriage...your non-judgmental way you presented your sermon and your admission to keeping gays out of the church was very heartfelt. We are all sinners and...gays should be welcomed in the church as sinners as all other sinners are.[7]

I believe more than a few Bills are out there hungering for a compassionate yet truthful treatment of homosexuality and a godly perspective on sexual sin. Confusion about God's view of sex is palpable even within the evangelical community.

A few years ago a carefully controlled study was done of nearly thirty-five hundred men and women who claimed to be conservative, evangelical, Bible-believing Christians. When asked about their attitude toward sex, three categories were identified: traditional, relational, and recreational.

The *traditional* group said that religious belief always guides their sexual behavior and that premarital, extramarital, and homosexual sex are wrong. The *relational* group stated sex should be a part of a loving relationship, but should not necessarily be restricted to marriage. The *recreational* group asserted that sex should be enjoyed for its own sake and didn't necessarily have anything to do with love.[8] The bombshell: According to this study, only 50.5 percent of conservative evangelicals fall into the traditional category. Half of evangelical Christians believe that sex does not necessarily have to be restricted to marriage.[9]

Furthermore, when sexuality is narrowed down to homosexuality, the discussion becomes more complex and controversial. A former consensus view of homosexuality has now morphed into a cultural battle the likes of which has not been seen in America since the civil rights movement of the sixties.[10]

Today the politics of personal destruction strives to silence any voice raised against homosexuality and gay marriage with a barrage of ad hominem attacks designed to shift the debate and put critics on the defensive. It is the kiss of death to be labeled homophobic, intolerant, prejudiced, outdated, or exclusive.[11] Still, we are compelled to speak where God speaks, and an answer to one of the most frequently asked questions deserves an answer.

---

When it comes to all sexual questions,
the big question is, Who makes the rules?

---

I begin with this foundational principle: *Sex is God's invention for all people, and sex is God's intention for most people.* Neither Christ-followers nor the church should hesitate in addressing anything that God created, because everything that God created is good. God, not Hollywood nor Hugh Hefner, created sex. But here's the rub: Because God created it, He sets the rules for when it is right and who can practice it. When you break those rules, you pay.

When it comes to all sexual questions, the big question is, Who makes the rules? If we make the rules then anything goes—homosexuality, polygamy, group sex, wife swapping, one-night stands, fornication, whatever. But if God makes the rules, then what He says goes, and God has plenty to say on the subject.

One principle continually rises to the top when we carefully examine the biblical view of sex. It is seen from a pronouncement in a garden in Genesis to a sermon on a hillside in Matthew to a letter written from a sex-crazed city in Greece. *Sex is best when sex is right, and sex is right when enjoyed in marriage between a husband and wife.*

No sin is quite like sexual sin. When you go beyond the boundaries laid down by the God who invented sex, it has a negative influence greater than almost any other sin. Yes, in one sense all sin is sin, but not all sin is the same. All sin brings equal condemnation, but not all sin brings equal consequences. The apostle Paul puts it this way: "Flee from sexual immorality. All other sins a person commits are outside the body, but whoever sins sexually, sins against their own body."[12]

Paul's words remind us of an important principle as we deal with this sensitive and increasingly volatile subject. God plays no favorites when it comes to sexual sin. Homosexuality is no greater sin than fornication or adultery. We must avoid the temptation to turn a blind eye to sexual sins we consider to be at least not "perverted." All sin is a perversion in God's eyes. Still, even the anatomical makeup of the male and female body tells us that homosexuality brings an unnaturalness into play not found in heterosexuality.[13]

Sadly, for the reasons mentioned above, more and more political and spiritual leaders are saying less and less about homosexuality, which has become the third rail for some politicians, professors, and pastors. *Time* magazine asked a famous pastor, who has become one of the leaders of the emergent church, his position on homosexuality. His response: "You know what, the thing that breaks my heart is that there's no way I can answer it without hurting someone on either side."[14]

Later in a story for another journal, he wrote,

> I hesitate in answering "the homosexual question" not because I am a cowardly flip-flopper who wants to tickle ears, but because I am a pastor, and pastors have learned from Jesus that there is more to answering a question than being right or even honest: we must also be...pastoral...
>
> Frankly, many of us don't know what we should think about homosexuality. We've heard all sides, but no position has yet won our confidence so that we can say "it seems good to the Holy Spirit and to us."[15]

I do not share this pastor's uncertainty. I may be wrong, but I am not in doubt about what I believe and what I understand God's Word teaches about homosexuality and gay marriage.

Still, what cannot be denied is the radical change that has occurred in what we as a nation and as a culture think and believe about homosexuality. It has gone from being condemned to condoned to confirmed as an appropriate moral lifestyle. This chapter unapologetically and unequivocally goes against this cultural grain.

Note from the outset that I am dealing with homosexual *practice*, for which a person is responsible, and not homosexual *preference*, for which a person may not be responsible. I am not talking about a person's condition; I am talking about a person's conduct. Also, I hope you will give this chapter a fair reading with an open mind. There may be some surprises awaiting those on both sides of this issue.

## Consult the Instructions

The first job I ever had was working in a "five and dime store" (today's equivalent would be a Dollar Tree store).[16] I had been hired at the beginning of the Christmas holidays and was immediately given the job of putting bicycles together. I experienced all the symptoms of a major heart attack. I had never put anything together in my life. I was born with two left hands, and I often tell people that if I had been Noah, everybody would have drowned.

I opened the first box and poured out all the parts, and staring at that mass of metal I may as well have been asked to build a 747 from scratch. Two hours later, I had made a unicycle out of a bicycle. When the manager came upstairs and saw the mess I had made, he exploded and asked me one question that taught me a lifelong lesson I have never forgotten: "Did you read the instructions?" Once I did, I had a clear picture in my mind of how the pieces fit together. Eventually I became a whiz at assembling bicycles.

Likewise, when it comes to all sexually related questions, we must "read the instructions" given by the God who gave us the gift of sex to begin with. Homosexuality must be seen in the light of the positive teaching in Scripture about human sexuality and the role of sex in society.

Three things are true about every person on this earth regardless of their sexual preference or their sexual identity: (1) We are all created humans, (2) we are all created sexual humans, (3) we are all created in the image of God. From the time God created the human race, He created us as sexual creatures with the ability and authority to have sexual relations both for procreation and pleasure. *But the ability to have sex was always meant to be under God's authority.* All sex was to be according to His plan and within His boundaries. That plan is clearly given in the creation account in the second chapter of Genesis.

> Our sexual desires are rooted in creation. From the beginning of time, God created sex as an expression of love to be experienced between a man and a woman.

Genesis 2:7 informs us that God formed the first man out of the dust of the earth and named him Adam. Interestingly, when He creates the second person, it was not from dust as you might expect. Here is what we read instead: "So the LORD God caused the man to fall into a deep sleep; and while he was sleeping, he took one of the man's ribs and then closed up the place with flesh. Then the LORD God made a woman from the rib he had taken out of the man, and he brought her to the man."[17]

When God created Eve out of Adam's flesh, He made a powerful statement about all sexuality. He separated femininity out of masculinity, forming two separate people. Out of one came two, and ever since then, there has been that implanted desire in the male and the female for those two to become one again in the intimacy of a sexual relationship.

Our sexual desires are rooted in creation. From the beginning of time, God created sex as an expression of love to be experienced between a man and a woman—but not just *any* man or woman. Scripture records where and when this sexual union is to take place: "That is why a man leaves his father and mother and is united to his wife, and they become one flesh."[18]

---

Idolatry allows you to customize your own god and actually play god yourself. If you play god, you can change the rules at any time to suit your preference, public opinion, or a particular situation.

---

Pretty much everything one needs to know about God's prescription for sex and marriage is found in that verse. First, God brings marriage partners together. Ministers may perform ceremonies, but God is the one who does weddings. Second, marriage is to be between two people, specifically a man and woman, who are to leave their parents in a public ceremony, signifying a new family unit is being formed by the husband and wife. Third, both partners in the marriage are to be permanently united in a heterosexual relationship that is sealed by sexual intercourse, which is where they become one flesh.

The Bible approves of no other kind of marriage or sexual intercourse. There is no alternative.

## Train Off the Tracks

But as the scriptural narrative continues, the human race deviates from God's standard. It is not long before laws are written prohibiting adultery, fornication, and homosexuality. Most people who are even vaguely familiar with the Old Testament are aware of the adultery of David, the polygamy of Solomon, and the rape of Tamar, but those were specifically heterosexual sins. The question arises, How did homosexuality come about? Where did the idea of sex between two people of the same gender arise?

In the apostle Paul's letter to fellow believers in Rome, he gives the theological explanation in the most exhaustive treatment of homosexuality in the New Testament:

> Because of this, God gave them over to shameful lusts. Even their women exchanged natural sexual relations for unnatural ones. In the same way the men also abandoned natural relations with women and were inflamed with lust for one another. Men committed shameful acts with other men, and received in themselves the due penalty for their error.[19]

What is the "this" that Paul says caused people to indulge in homosexual practice? It was idolatry. Paul is talking about people who "exchanged the glory of the immortal God for images made to look like a mortal human being and birds and animals and reptiles."[20]

What is idolatry? Idolatry is replacing the real God with any false god. Why is the human heart so inclined toward idolatry? Why do we want to worship self-made gods instead of the one and only true God? The reason is simple: If you create your own god, then your god can make the rules. Since that god is your creation, he is under your authority. Idolatry allows you to customize your own god and actually play god yourself. If you play god, you can change the rules at any time to suit your preference, public opinion, or a particular situation.

Paul is describing those who have received, rejected, and replaced the knowledge of the true God with the god of their own creation.

Then Paul records God's response with a phrase he repeats three times: "God gave them over."[21]

When people decided to exchange the real God for a false god, they also agreed to exchange heterosexual intercourse for homosexual intercourse.[22] That is why the Bible condemns homosexual acts as sin, because those acts are expressions of the greatest sin of all, which is idolatry. This sheds light on a passage of Scripture that lists certain types of sinners who will not be allowed to spend eternity with God:

> Or do you not know that wrongdoers will not inherit the kingdom of God? Do not be deceived: Neither the sexually immoral nor *idolaters* nor adulterers nor men who have sex with men nor thieves nor the greedy nor drunkards nor slanderers nor swindlers will inherit the kingdom of God.[23]

Don't miss the idolatry reference immediately following sexual immorality and preceding specific sexual sins. It is a connection that is both causative and prescriptive. Homosexuality is a result of an incipient idolatry, and idolatry gives "pseudo-divine" sanction to sexual sin.

But one might ask, "What about people who are born gay?" This argument is used frequently to bolster the claim that God made homosexuals to be homosexuals, and therefore there can be nothing wrong with it. If the writers of Scripture had known that homosexuality is not a chosen behavior but an orientation dictated from birth by genetic predisposition, the argument goes, they would have written something entirely differently. So a great debate rages whether homosexual practice is a product of nature or nurture.

I have neither time nor space to fully address this argument. There are many resources one can study to see how tenuous the evidence is for this assertion.[24] Still, one quote from a research scientist with a PhD in biochemistry is worth noting:

> Science has not yet discovered any genetically dictated behavior in humans. So far, genetically dictated behaviors of the one-gene-one-trait variety have been found only in simple organisms…But if many genes are involved in a behavior, then changes in that behavior will tend to take place slowly and steadily (say, changes of a few percent each generation over many generations, perhaps thirty). That being so, homosexuality could not appear and disappear suddenly in family trees the way it does.[25]

But an even greater response to this argument is this: It is irrelevant. Nobody gets a free pass from God for rebellious behavior regardless of where or how that desire arises. We are responsible for our behavior even if it is genetically motivated. Suppose we find a kleptomaniac gene or a murderer gene or an alcoholic gene? Would that excuse theft or murder or alcoholism? Everyone on planet earth has been born with a genetic predisposition to sin,[26] but that does not excuse our sinful behavior.

Also, as with all sin, there are consequences inherent in the homosexual lifestyle also borne out by Scripture: "Men committed shameful acts with other men, and received in themselves the due penalty for their error."[27]

---

We are to treat all people as fellow human beings whom God loves and for whom Jesus Christ died. In short, we are to treat them with love itself.

---

Most of the sexual activities the majority of homosexuals engage in are physiologically unnatural and, in many cases, physically destructive. It is not coincidental that homosexual men are eight times more likely to contract hepatitis and fourteen times more likely to contract syphilis, and that homosexuality accounts for 80 percent of the serious sexually transmitted diseases in the United States. Additionally, the psychological toll on homosexual men makes them six times more likely than heterosexual men to attempt suicide.[28]

The picture that Hollywood and the media paint of homosexuality as just an alternative lifestyle is more than a little photoshopped. The life expectancy of a homosexual is a full two decades shorter than that of the public at large.[29] If we are going to be truthful and loving, we must inform the homosexual that this chosen lifestyle is neither a healthy, nor a holy, nor (for many) even a happy one.

## Marriage: Only Brides and Grooms May Apply

One no longer has the luxury of addressing the homosexual issue apart from gay marriage. Contrary to the perception perpetrated by many, the opposition to same-sex marriage is not about hate but about debate. Additionally, the argument about gay marriage is not really about gays. It is really an argument about marriage. Gay marriage is not about extending marriage as we know it; it is about ending marriage as we know it.

Neither homosexuals nor heterosexuals can deny that the only way that marriage can be extended to gays is to fundamentally change the meaning of marriage. Across countries and cultures, marriage has been universally defined as heterosexual in nature.[30] The dirty secret is that once marriage is redefined in such a fundamental way, it ceases to mean anything at all. One expert on marriage put it this way:

> Some marital practices have changed with culture and time, but the procreational form of marriage is not a social construct and has never changed. Marriage precedes culture because the existence of society depends on marriage (not the other way around). Every civilization through history

has recognized the procreational structure of marriage bridging the male-female divide…the procreational form of marriage cannot be denied without destroying marriage.[31]

If marriage is redefined as being no longer the union of one man and one woman, but rather any two persons who want to cohabit, why not have a marriage of three people? What is wrong with polygamy—one man with two wives or ten or one wife with twelve husbands? We are back to the question, Who makes the rules?

For all of human history until recently, there was an acknowledgment across civilizations and cultures that marriage was meaningful and has an unchanging meaning—it is a union between a man and a woman for the purpose of building a stable home and having children.

This is the answer to the question, "What's wrong with allowing those who don't accept what the Bible says about marriage or the traditional meaning of marriage to marry? Why can't we just live and let live?" One glaring and fundamental reason stands out. Once the definition of marriage is changed, marriage as an institution is both permanently devalued and its meaning destroyed. That is a consequence that affects everyone.

For example, suppose the culture decides that the word *red* should no longer be restricted to describing the color that has traditionally been thought of as red; instead, *red* can now be used to describe something that is blue or black or purple or green or yellow. A peach is now red. A daisy is now red. Grass is now red. You've just emptied red of any meaning and any purpose whatsoever. Furthermore, think of what would happen at traffic lights. You have just affected me and my welfare.

Imagine you are on a boat trying to get to the other side of a lake, and one man insists that he has a right to drill a hole through the bottom of his side of the boat. You tell him he can't do that, but he says,

"What does my side of the boat have to do with your side of the boat? Just stay on your side and I'll stay on mine." When the water begins to seep into that boat, like it or not, you are going to find out that what one person does on his side of the boat affects everybody in the boat. Allowing gay marriage detrimentally affects marriage as an institution as well as every person who married "by the rules."

Still, this is a moot point for this reason: If homosexuality is wrong, then homosexual marriage must also be wrong.

---

The Bible unequivocally condemns homosexuality. But it condemns a lot of other things, such as gossip, greed, bitterness, and hypocrisy, that have caused me a whole lot more trouble than have homosexuals.

---

Additionally, we haven't even taken into account the consensus view that children function best in a stable environment where both a father and a mother are present. Children need a mother so they can understand how to relate to the feminine side of life and a father to learn how to relate to the masculine side of life. Don't take my word for it. Princeton University sociologist Sara McLanahan said,

> If we were asked to design a system for making sure that chil-
> dren's basic needs were met, we would probably come up
> with something quite similar to the two-parent ideal. Such
> a design in theory would not only ensure that children had
> access to the time and money of two adults, but it would
> also provide a system of checks and balances that promoted
> quality parenting. The fact that both parents have a biolog-
> ical connection to the child would increase the likelihood
> that the parents would identify with the child and be will-
> ing to sacrifice for that child, and it would reduce the likeli-
> hood that either parent would abuse the child.[32]

## Amazing Grace for All

I have admittedly approached this subject with what some may see as cold logic indifferent to the needs and hurts of homosexuals, both inside and outside the church. I hope with my closing words to correct that perception. We are to treat people, regardless of their class, color, nationality, or sexual preference, as fellow human beings whom God loves and for whom Jesus Christ died. In short, we are to treat them with love itself.

I confess, both as a pastor and a devoted follower of Christ, that for too long the Christian community has made the homosexual the whipping boy for sin. Yes, homosexual activity is a sin. The Bible unequivocally condemns it. But it condemns a lot of other things, such as gossip, greed, bitterness, and hypocrisy, that have caused me a whole lot more trouble than have homosexuals.

> Rather than sunbathe in the light of our own self-righteousness, we need to honestly and humbly start talking about the sins we tolerate in our own lives and the lives of our churches.

We should not single out homosexual activity for special condemnation. The reason I included a chapter on it in this book is that it has become one of the questions I am asked most frequently. Every kind of sexual relationship and activity that falls outside the boundary of the marriage bed between a husband and a wife is equally sin in the eyes of God. That includes polygamy, cohabitation, adultery, one-night stands, and divorce.

Rather than sunbathe in the light of our own self-righteousness, we need to honestly and humbly start talking about the sins we tolerate in our own lives and the lives of our churches. We must get away from a double standard that places the sin of homosexuality in a different category than adultery or fornication. We must pull the plank out of our own eye even as we pull the splinter out of the eyes of others.

We must become havens of hope and givers of grace to the homosexuals who come into our churches looking for love and mercy rather than condemnation and judgment. No, we do not shy away from the truth about any sin, but we aggressively seek out every person, heterosexual or homosexual, as the Shepherd seeks the lost sheep and the Father awaits the lost son. The church should be the first place the homosexual looks for grace and love, not the last.

If you are one of those who struggles with homosexuality, you need to know that belief can be changed and behavior can be changed. In fact, belief determines behavior (or at least it should). If you change your belief and understand what God says about homosexuality, then God can change your behavior.

I have seen it happen. I saw it with two lesbians who visited a church I pastored several years ago. It was obvious to all when they walked in that they were lesbians, right down to who played the male role and who played the female role. I made it a point to be the one to visit them later that week. As I sat on the floor playing with the daughter of one of the women, I tackled the issue head on.

"Let's not pretend we don't know what we're dealing with here," I said. "I realize you are a lesbian couple, and I am here to love you and answer any questions you have." They had only one. "Are we welcome in your church?" I was ashamed it was a question they felt they needed to ask and I needed to answer.

"Absolutely," I replied. "But know that we preach God's truth unequivocally, and His Word says that your lifestyle is wrong. I won't go out of my way to mention the topic in my preaching because of your presence, but neither will I try to avoid it for the same reason. But we want you to come to our church."

They thanked me, and as I started to leave, I said, "God loves you just the way you are." They loved that. And then I said, "But He loves you too much to let you stay that way." Then I shared the gospel of Christ and His grace with them and left.

I repeatedly went back over several months, and finally one day, as I went into their backyard to share with them, they were both smiling. "We have given up our lifestyle—we want to receive Jesus Christ," they said. I will never forget the joy of seeing those ladies get on their knees and make the greatest decision any human will ever make.

But even more poignant is the memory of one of the ladies coming to my church office on a nasty, thunderstorm-filled day. She came to thank me for caring enough to tell her the truth about her sin and about God's love. She said, "I don't miss that old lifestyle because I sure do love my new one!"

> Love is the message homosexuals need to
> hear and the ministry they need to feel from
> a church grateful for God's amazing grace.

I was reminded of the words Paul penned in a letter to a church in Corinth—a sex-crazed city that would be rated XXX even by today's lax standards. That church was made up of one rough crowd: former sexual reprobates, adulterers, male prostitutes, and homosexuals, not to mention thieves, drunkards, slanderers, and swindlers. But somehow they made it to this Christian outpost in this spiritual desert, and Paul reminded them of the transformation they had experienced when they came to Christ: "And that is what some of you were. But you were washed, you were sanctified, you were justified in the name of the Lord Jesus Christ and by the Spirit of our God."[33]

All of us were *something we should not have been at one time in our lives*. But God is in the life-changing business.

No homosexual has a monopoly on sin. We cannot cast the first stone, the second stone, or even the third stone at homosexuals. We have to love them and we should love them because Jesus loved them. We should love them, not because of what they are or what they do, but because of what they can become in the Lord Jesus Christ.

Remember my friend Bill from Wisconsin? I got this follow-up email from him after I had already submitted my original draft of this chapter:

> [Pastor]: I can't begin to tell you how much the "H" bomb sermon did for me. I joined a Bible church and was baptized January 20. The pastor here gives me private Bible study every week. The longer I am in the Word, the less I want to sway into temptation. I did a four-hour testimony of my whole entire life. There were many tears and disclosures in that four hours. I am now leading a completely chaste and celibate life. Please pass on to other homosexual men and women that reading and studying the Word will bring them freedom and liberation and closer to the Holy Spirit. My friend, I thank you so much.
>
> Bill

In an interview with Billy Graham on *20/20*, the TV host asked, "If you had a homosexual child, would you love him?" Dr. Graham responded without missing a beat, "I would love that one even more."

Love is the message homosexuals need to hear and the ministry they need to feel from a church grateful for God's amazing grace. Can the "Bills" hear you?

# CHAPTER EIGHT

# Do You Really Have a Plan for My Life? If So, How Do I Find It?

From the time I was five years old, I knew what I wanted to do with my life (the operative word is "I"). I wanted to be a lawyer. I had a keen interest in American history, the U.S. Constitution, the law, and American government. Don't ask me why; no one in my family had ever been a lawyer. But I was determined to be the first.

I had crafted my future perfectly. I graduated from high school and went to college, where I chose to major in accounting. "Chose" carries with it the same nuance as "I chose to drink goat urine." For the most part, I miserably endured the sheer tediousness of accounting. (How many suave, debonair accountants do *you* know?)

But remember, *I had a plan for my life*. I was going to take my accounting degree, merge it with my law degree, and become a crack corporate attorney proficient at everything from money to mergers.

*Ministry?* Wasn't even on the radar screen. I wasn't interested in saving anyone; I wanted to sue them.

Then it was as if God said, "I interrupt your regular programming for this important announcement: I have some bad news and I have some good news." The bad news was that I wasn't going to law school. The good news was that I was going to graduate school—to seminary. The bad news was, I would never practice law before any judge. The good news was, I was going to preach God's law for the Ultimate Judge. The bad news was, my dreams of becoming financially independent by the time I was forty were gone. The good news was (unknown to me at the time) that I would live a far richer life than I would have had I missed God's will for my life.

So instead of preparing another legal brief, executing another merger, or perhaps arguing a case before the Supreme Court (another one of my goals), I am banging away on my Mac with another God-given opportunity to have an eternal impact on someone's life by ministering God's truth through the written word. More importantly, I have the incredible satisfaction of knowing I have followed God's plan for my life.

---

God does indeed have a will for your life.

---

I want you to think about *who you are* at this moment. I don't mean just your name, but who you really are as a person. Then I want you to think about *what you are*. I don't mean just your race or your gender. I mean what you do for a living, what your vocation may be, what you spend most of your time doing, and what consumes most of your thinking. Finally, I want you to think about *where you are* in your life—vocationally, financially, relationally, and spiritually.

Now a dash of cold-water reality: You are who you are, what you are, and where you are right now, for the most part, because of one thing—the choices and decisions you have made. That doesn't mean that you are responsible for the choices others make in response to your choices, but your choices always shape where you are in life.

Bottom line, life is nothing more than a series of decisions. Your major in college, the person you married, the number of kids you have, the work you do, and the place you live are all a result of your choice and your decision.

We've all made two types of decisions in our lives: good and bad. If you are like me, you would like to have some of your decisions back. We would all love do-overs. For us golfers, we would all like some mulligans for some of the decisions we've made.

It would be wonderful if we could always make the right decision, exercise the right choice, and do the right thing. Good news: *God wants to help you make those kinds of choices and decisions in your life.* The way He does that is by revealing His will for you. But that raises the big question: "How do you know God's will?"

Allow me to ask you some questions:

- Are you struggling to know God's will in some area of your life right now?

- Do you have a desire to know God's will and to do it once you know it?

- Are you tired of making bad choices because you have been executing your plan for your life, not His?

- Are you facing a crucial decision right now, and you really want to make sure you get it right?

Then I know God's will for you at this moment: it's to read this chapter.

## God Has a Plan

Let's begin with some facts concerning God's will. First, *God does indeed have a will for your life.* The apostle Paul wrote these words to some believers struggling with this issue: "Be very careful, then, how you live—not as unwise but as wise, making the most of every opportunity, because the days are evil. Therefore do not be foolish, but understand what the Lord's will is."[1]

You can live life only two ways: wisely and unwisely. The wise way to live is in the center of God's will. The foolish way is to live outside of God's will.

Furthermore, that passage commands us to "understand what the Lord's will is." Time is brief. Life is short. You get one shot to do it right, and God knows that better than you do. God wants you to get the biggest bang for the buck while you are on this planet. He has invested life in you, and He wants the biggest return He can get on His investment. The way He maximizes His investment in you, and the way you maximize your time on this earth, is to be in the center of His will.

So it stands to reason that God wants to reveal His will to you and He wants you to know it. God wants you to know His will even more than you want to know it. He doesn't play games with us. He doesn't play hide-and-seek. He doesn't say, "OK—you're getting warmer," or "Nope—you're getting colder." No, He has a plan for us to discover His plan. He has a way for us to discover His will.

## Clarify Then Specify

Before we get into the specifics of finding God's will, a point of clarification. Every time you read in the Bible such phrases as "the Lord's will," "the will of God," "the will of the Lord," or "God's will," it is used in three basic ways.

First, the Bible speaks of God's *providential will*. This can be referred to as God's sovereign will, determined will, immutable will, or unchangeable will. This is the will of God that overrides all human decisions. God has sovereignly determined that certain things are going to happen, and nobody can change them.

A simple example of this was the death of Jesus Christ. Jesus was born not only to die but to die specifically on a cross. He would die that way and no other. Looking back on an event he witnessed, Peter said, "This man was handed over to you by God's deliberate plan and foreknowledge; and you, with the help of wicked men, put him to death by nailing him to the cross."[2]

Jesus was the invincible man until the cross, for it was in the providential will of God that He die in that place at that time in that way.

"The will of God" at other times refers to God's *practical will*. This is also known as the *moral will* of God. God has a moral will that He wants us to follow, and His moral will is universal for all times, all places, and all people. The ultimate example would be the Ten Commandments. Since those were given, it always has been and always will be wrong to lie, steal, commit adultery, or to covet what someone else has. One verse gives a perfect example of this: "It is God's will that you should be sanctified: that you should avoid sexual immorality.[3]

Little if any of what God desires for our behavior, conduct, ethics, and morality is left to chance or guesswork.

Finally, "the will of God" is used in a third way that refers to God's *personal will*. This is God's will for us in the many decisions we all face. It is also this aspect of God's will that we usually struggle with the most. Do I take that job or this one? Do I go to this college or that college? Do I date this person or not? Should I invest my money with this person or that person? Should I make this purchase or not? Is this the person I should marry? These are the decisions we wish were spelled out in Scripture, but they are not. All we can say is that God's will for us is to proactively seek this part of His will.

How do we find His will in these everyday decisions? Is it behind curtain number one, curtain number…well, you get the picture. I know a lot of us wish that God would just tell us; we would love to hear a deep bass voice speak out loud and let us know what He wants us to do.

---

We can know with certainty in any crucial situation God's will for our lives. God has given us certain tools and instructions on how to make wise decisions that we can be confident are in the flow of His will.

---

I believe I did hear God speak out loud one time, but it happened only once and has never happened again. Strangely enough, it happened on a golf course. I was playing my very first round of golf and had come to a hole with a large water trap. I had bought some new balls and didn't want to lose any of them, so I took out a real old ball. I teed the ball up and was about to hit it when this voice came out of nowhere: "James, where is your faith? Take out a new ball." I was scared to death. I went to my golf bag and took out a brand new ball. I teed it up, and the voice said, "James, give me your best practice swing." I stepped back and gave my best practice swing. The voice came back and said, "James, take out the old ball."

OK, that didn't really happen. And as a general rule God does not speak audibly. But I do believe that God still speaks, and I believe He speaks clearly. I believe that we can know with certainty in any crucial situation God's will for our lives. God has given us certain tools and instructions on how to make wise decisions that we can be confident are in the flow of His will.

## Some Basic Assumptions

One of the most familiar verses in the book of Proverbs outlines both our part and God's part in knowing His will:

> Trust in the LORD with all your heart
> and lean not on your own understanding;
> in all your ways acknowledge him,
> and he will make your paths straight.[4]

We are told specifically that if we do two things and refrain from one thing, God will do *His* thing and direct our paths or "make [our] paths straight." First, we are told to trust Him with all our heart. God reveals His will only to those who wholeheartedly trust in Him. Sounds simple enough, but there is more to this than saying, "I believe in God." You cannot know God's will until you know God, and you can know Him only through His Son Jesus Christ. God says it is His will for all to have this relationship with Christ.[5]

Once you take that step of following God's will by trusting Jesus Christ completely for your eternal life, then you can begin to trust God for His will in this life.

Again, the word *trust* means more than believing. It means to trust to the point of complete obedience. Trust is saying yes to whatever God wants you to do, even before you know what that is. It's the trust of a child who jumps from a tree believing his father will catch him.

We finally get to the heart of the problem most of us have with God's will. The real problem is not in *finding* God's will. The real problem is *doing* it.

Two questions are always asked whenever we're on a quest for God's will. One is our question and one is God's. Our question is, "God, what do You want me to do?" His question is, "Will you do what I want you to do?" Then we play the "you go first" game. We want God to tell us what He wants us to do first and make that just one of the options we will consider. But God won't go first. God will not show us His will until we say, "All systems go."

God wants you to sign a blank contract, and then He will fill in the details. You have to first agree you are going to do His will no matter what it is, even if it means changing your major, leaving your boyfriend, staying with your wife or husband, taking another job, or even refusing another job.

That is why we must not "lean on our own understanding." We must not try to figure everything out on our own. How often do we immediately ask this question when facing a difficult decision: "What do I think I ought to do?" We shouldn't lean on either our logic or our feelings. Our first resource and our first look must be to God.

---

God's will is not a mystery and it is not mystical.
God wants you to know His will more
than you want to know it.

---

The reason is simple. An ancient prophet reminds us "that our lives are not our own. We are not able to plan our own course."[6] There is no way you can run your life, make your own decisions, and really get it right for this simple reason—you don't know the future. You don't know all the ripples your decisions are going to make. But God does. Because God knows the future, God knows what is going to be best for your future. That is why He should always be your first resource, not your last resort when facing a difficult decision.

Then we are told to "acknowledge him in all our ways." Today, to acknowledge something often means to pay lip service to its reality by a nod of the head, a wink of the eye, or a polite smile. In the Hebrew language, the word that has been translated "acknowledge" goes far deeper. It means to "focus on something and follow it." We can translate it, "In all your ways focus on God and follow Him." Your ways are your actions. They are the moral choices you make every day when you decide whether you are going to do right or wrong. It is following the practical will of God for your life.

You can know God's *personal will* only if you are following His *practical* or *moral will*. Only when you are doing what you know you should be doing today can you know God's will for tomorrow. God reveals His unknown will only to those who are already practicing His known will. If you are disobedient in a moral area of your life (God's practical will), you will not receive guidance in personal areas of your life (God's personal will).

The *known will of God* is what you discover by reading His Word, knowing His character, and studying His ways. These are the things you know you are supposed to be doing. The *unknown will of God* involves future choices and decisions where you seek His guidance. When you daily obey the known will of God, you will then be in a position to know the unknown will of God.

God's will is not a mystery and it is not mystical. God wants you to know His will more than you want to know it. But you won't know it until you (a) want to do it more than anything else, and (b) you are following what you know His will is for your life right now.

When you are living out God's practical will He will show you His personal will. But if you don't He won't. Are you looking for God's person for you to marry? Then don't engage in premarital sex. Are you looking for God to direct you in your business decisions? Then don't lie, don't cheat, and don't turn in false income-tax returns. Do you want God's blessing on your marriage and on your children? Then, be faithful to your spouse. Don't be flirting with the people you work with.

Stay away from pornography. Put yourself in a position, morally, to be able to hear God's voice.

Once we do our part, then God promises to do His, which is to "direct our paths."

## How God Speaks

Up to this point in the Proverbs 3 passage, it has all been about what we are to do. The ball is in our court. But once we've done our part, we're told that God "will make our paths straight." That phrase can also be translated "direct our path." When we are trying to decide which path to take, God will give us the one thing we need—direction.

Let's face it—when it comes to the future, we are all blind. When it comes to tomorrow, we are all in the dark. If we knew ahead of time how every decision would turn out, we would know what decision to make. We don't know, of course, but God does, and He longs to lead us, direct us, and make sure we get on the right path.

He has not given us a crystal ball we can consult, nor is His MO some sign in the sky or an audible voice, though some try to find His will that way. Instead, He has given us a box of tools tailor-made to help us discern His will in those tough decisions we all face.

---

The Bible doesn't specifically direct us to a certain college to attend or a certain companion to marry. It does give principles and guidelines that help us eliminate certain choices and consider others.

---

One of the funniest stories I ever heard my dad tell was about a man in our little country church who believed God had called him to preach. Occasionally when the pastor was away, he would let this man preach, and he displayed no evidence of any divine calling. His sermons were great for anyone suffering from insomnia. After this man set the Guinness World Record for the most boring sermon in history, my dad remarked to several men, "If he's a preacher, I'm an astronaut." Well, Dad's ill-placed assessment got back to this man.

The next Sunday he approached my dad and said, "Glenn, I understand that you don't believe it's God's will for me to preach."

"I really don't," my dad said.

"Let me tell you why I know it's God's will for me to become a preacher."

"Go ahead," Dad said.

"I was out working in my garden, and I looked up in the clouds and saw three letters—GPC. I knew immediately that those three letters meant Go Preach Christ."

"That's not what those three letters meant," my dad said without batting an eye.

"Well, what did they mean?"

"Go pick cotton."

Placing secret messages in the clouds is not the way God operates— then or now. God has provided certain tools to help us determine His will when we are presented with many options and to decide when to walk through an open door and when not to.

## Tools to Help Us Determine God's Will

The first tool is any *biblical principle* that may relate to our situation. The Bible doesn't specifically direct us to a certain city to live in, a certain college to attend, or a certain companion to marry. At the same time, the Bible does give principles and guidelines that help us eliminate certain choices and consider others. One principle to remember is this: *God's direction will never contradict God's instruction.*

It doesn't matter if someone has a crystal ball and you see with your own eyes a spirit telling you to do something or go somewhere—if you know it's against the Word of God, you say no. As Isaiah the prophet warned the people of Israel,

> When someone tells you to consult mediums and spiritists, who whisper and mutter, should not a people inquire of their God? Why consult the dead on behalf of the living? Consult God's instruction and the testimony of warning. If anyone does not speak according to this word, they have no light of dawn.[7]

The way God most often uses His Word to guide us is through understanding biblical principles. The Bible is not primarily a bunch of rules; it is a collection of principles. These are general guidelines that give us discernment and wisdom to understand what God would have us to do. The psalmist said, "Teach me knowledge and good judgment, for I trust your commands."[8]

---

Wise counselors help you to avoid the most dangerous way to try to perceive God's will and that is through your feelings.

---

This is why it is so important to be a student of God's Word. The more you understand Scripture, the better you will know God. The primary purpose of reading the Bible is not to know the Bible but to know God. The better you know God, the better you know His character. The better you know His character, the more you know what He wants and how He acts. The better you know what He wants and how He acts, the more you understand His commands. The more you understand His commands, the easier it is to discern His counsel.

One question always worth asking when choosing a course of

action is, "Does God's Word prohibit or permit what I am thinking about doing?"

The second tool God uses is *wise people*. The wisest man who ever lived (outside of Jesus, of course) said, "Plans fail for lack of counsel, but with many advisers they succeed."[9] The best way to keep from getting out on the limb of a bad decision is to make sure you consult several wise, godly counselors.

I cannot overemphasize this principle enough. Wise counselors help you to avoid the most dangerous way to try to perceive God's will and that is through your feelings. I cringe whenever I hear people say, "I just feel this is what God wants me to do." Usually, the reason you feel that God wants you to do something is because of some other feeling that's motivating you. Let me explain.

Some of the worst decisions I have ever made came out of a *feeling* I should do something. One of the worst hires I ever made was to put a person in a key position in our church because I really liked him and he went out of his way to make me feel good. It turned out to be a disaster.

That principle is even more critical when *negative feelings* are driving the decision. Never make a decision to do something if any of the following feelings are involved: undeserved guilt, unresolved anger, or unsettled anxiety. If you do something as a knee-jerk reaction just because someone put you on a guilt trip, that is not the will of God.

If you make up your mind you're going to do something because you are angry at someone and you think you're exercising God's righteous indignation (when it's really your own bitterness), don't do it. If you do something because you are worried that the opportunity will be gone forever if you don't—that most likely is a poor reason to proceed. Remember, just because something *seems* right doesn't automatically make it right. Another proverb says, "The way of fools seems right to them, but the wise listen to advice."[10]

Failing to get wise counsel can be nothing short of disastrous. I know a couple who destroyed a twenty-year friendship because they made a hasty decision that wound up hurting three different families. When they informed their pastor, he wisely asked them, "Did you get any counsel before you made this decision?" They answered no. (The pastor was so dumbfounded by their response, he asked the question a second time.) Then he asked, "Can you both look me in the eye and tell me you believe this is God's will for your life?" The husband nodded after a brief hesitation, and the wife stared at the floor. Even sadder is that the decision was a reaction to a comment from a third party made in anger. Guilt drove the decision. All might have been avoided if wise counsel had been sought.

But getting counsel is not enough. God even wills that we choose *wise* counselors. You need to find individuals who have proven themselves to be wise, godly, loyal, trustworthy, and truthful. These people desire God's best for you. Most of the time, though not always, they will be older and more mature than you are.

To help you determine who would make good counselors, ask the following questions:

1. *Have they proven to be trustworthy in the past?* Have they proven that they will be honest and give you the best objective advice regardless of how painful it may be for you or them?

2. *Do they know all the facts?* Nobody can give you the best option until they know every option.

3. *Are they objective?* This is somewhat akin to the first qualification. Can this person be trusted to tell you what is best for you and all parties involved?

4. *In their own situation, are they where you want to be?* Never go for marriage counseling to someone who has been divorced four times. If you are struggling in your marriage, go to

someone with a strong marriage. If you are struggling with your kids, go to someone who has shown success raising their own.

Make sure you get advice from more than one person. There is wisdom in many counselors.[11] No one person has all the answers, and multiple counselors help to confirm good advice.

The third tool God uses is what I call *spiritual prompting*. One great advantage Christ-followers have is the inner guidance provided by the indwelling Holy Spirit. He functions as God's GPS to guide us in our decision making. As Paul told the church at Corinth, "What we have received is not the spirit of the world, but the Spirit who is from God, so that we may understand what God has freely given us."[12]

I have found in my own life that God uses the Scripture and the Spirit like guard rails. The Scripture protects us from purely *rational* decisions ("this is what I *think* I ought to do") while the Spirit protects us from purely emotional decisions ("this is what I *feel* I ought to do").

Several years ago I began thinking about leaving a church where I had been the pastor for almost eighteen years and planting a new church. I wasn't short on reasons not to do it. I was about to turn fifty, was deeply loved in my church, things were going well, and I was living in a velvet-covered comfort zone. Though I had been given an unbelievable opportunity, I had easily come up with at least ten or fifteen rock-solid reasons why I should not leave my church. On paper it seemed foolish and foolhardy. Frankly, I had almost talked myself out of doing what I knew was God's will for me. (I can testify that you can *think* you know God's will and be dead wrong if you haven't utilized all the tools previously mentioned.)

So much of what I was reading in Scripture was confirming to me I should start the new church, and counsel from others was tracking the same course. But rationally and emotionally I still fought alligators on every side. Still, I was praying constantly for God to show me His course of action.

In the midst of this agonizing time, I kept a doctor's appointment and sat in the waiting room, turning over in my mind all the wonderful reasons why I should not leave my cocoon of comfort. I yearned for a word from the Lord and was afraid I would hear it at the same time.

I randomly (I thought) picked up a magazine. It was a magazine for wealthy people, which is why I normally never read it. As I opened this magazine, a thought came to mind: *James, if you stay right where you are, you can coast the rest of your life.* The magazine fell open, and in the middle of the page in bold print were the words, "Remember—when you are coasting it is all downhill." I looked around to see if God was sitting right beside me. I knew at that moment that the Spirit of God was telling me, at a minimum, "Don't base your decision on your desire to coast."

There's nothing wrong with planning, thinking things through, getting out spreadsheets and charts, listing all the pros and cons, talking it over with others, and adding up the good and the bad. These can all be good and necessary steps. But you must also stay sensitive to the Spirit of God, believing that He will enable you to hear the voice of God and confirm in your heart the path you should choose. How does this take place? By using the last tool.

The final tool is *inner peace*. When you are in the center of God's will, you will find "the peace of God, which transcends all understanding" in your soul. This peace "will guard your hearts and your minds"[13] from doubting you are on the wrong path. I have found that this peace is God's way of saying, "I have directed your path, and you are headed for the right decision." You will find that *the will of God will never lead you where the peace of God will not keep you.*

Over twenty years ago I faced one of the most difficult decisions

I've ever grappled with. I had an opportunity to go to a church that had worldwide prestige. They were offering me more money than I'd ever dreamed I could make pastoring a church. They were going to put me in a house far beyond what I ever dreamed I would live in. The story of my dealings with this church even made it to *Time* magazine. (I still have about a thousand copies if you'd like to read one of them.)

In the midst of this situation, I got a call from Dr. Charles Stanley. "James," he said, "I know you're facing a crucial decision, and I just wanted to give you one piece of advice. If you are 99.99 percent sure you ought to do this, then don't do it."

"Why?" I said.

"Because when the first crisis comes, that .01 percent of doubt will kill you."

---

When you put God in His rightful place,
God will put you in the right place.

---

My youngest son, Joshua, is a pilot (and a great one at that), and I will always remember the first time I flew with him. I had (foolishly) promised him that I would be the first to go up with him as soon as he got his license. I'm not saying I was nervous or sorry for my hasty promise, but just as we were about to take off, I looked at him and said, "I just want you to know there's no one I would rather die with than you." Yes, I was as nervous as I would have been if I were about to have brain surgery and my doctor said just before I went under, "Pray for me—you're my first patient."

However, it didn't take me long to realize that Joshua had learned well and I was in good hands. As we were coming in for our landing, Joshua said, "Dad, I told you that the most critical point by far in a flight is the landing. Anybody can get up, but not everybody can get down." Then he told me to watch a battery of lights to the left of the runway. In aircraft lingo these lights are known as PAPI (Precision Approach Path Indicator). They are a great aid to a pilot when making a visual approach for landing.

For obvious reasons, angle of approach is critical to a pilot in landing an airplane. Too steep—you crash; too high—you miss the runway. PAPI, which consists of a bank of four lights that can glow red or white, provides the pilot with an accurate guide slope on final approach.[14] The lights will appear either white or red to the pilot depending on the position of the airplane relative to the specified angle of approach. The key is to make sure the red lights are over the white lights. That configuration ensures that you are on the right path for a safe landing.[15]

So for a pilot looking to be on the right path and arrive at his intended destination, the task is relatively simple: Make sure the lights line up just right and enjoy the landing.

I have discovered that when I have lined up key decisions with biblical principles, wise people, spiritual prompting, and an inner peace, I can rest assured that I have done all I can to be in the center of God's will. God does direct our paths.

Still, everything depends upon having a relationship with God through Christ and a completely surrendered will to His will. When you put God in His rightful place, God will put you in the right place. That doesn't mean life will always be easy or tough times won't come. It does mean that you will always be where God can protect you and provide for you as you walk in the paths He directs. If you do what you know to do when you know to do it, then He will reveal to you what you don't know to do when He wants you to do it.

Not long ago I was driving through a sleepy little town called Winder, Georgia. Teresa and I had been on an appointment, and as we were driving home, I realized we were passing the cemetery where my grandparents were buried. So we stopped to see their burial place. As I looked at their tombstones, I saw only a birth date, a death date, and a hyphen in between. For some reason, I began to focus not on their names or those dates but on that horizontal line separating the two.

A thought hit me broadside: That hyphen speaks volumes, for it represents a person's entire life and the sum total of the results of their choices and decisions. We tend to look at the two dates. God looks at the hyphen. That's where the real story is.

You and I are moving along that hyphen right now. Whether that hyphen represents a life well-lived or a life wasted depends on whether that life is lived in the center of God's will. As one of Jesus' best friends put it, "The world and its desires pass away, but whoever does the will of God lives forever."[16] To steal from an old advertising slogan: God's will—don't leave home without it.

# Some of Your Followers Keep Talking About Being "Born Again." What's With That?

We have all had it happen to us at least once—the dreaded knock on your front door. You open it to find to your dismay two (usually two, sometimes three) people standing at your door. You know instinctively that it is not Avon since (a) there is more than one, and (b) most often they are males. You also know almost instantaneously they are either a group out of Salt Lake City (often the bikes are a dead giveaway) or the ones who refer to themselves as "witnesses."

One of my staff got this knock on his door recently as he was headed out to work. Two pleasantly smiling people greeted him warmly (let's just say they weren't riding bicycles) and asked if they could come in.

Knowing he would be late for work, he almost refused. But something told him this was more important than being on time that day, so he invited them in.

J.W.,[1] the trainer, was using Tom (my staff member) to teach his trainee (evidently a recent convert) how to recruit people into the Kingdom. When they got onto the subject of the Kingdom, Tom pounced (if you know Tom, an apt metaphor).

"Have you studied the Kingdom of God?" Tom asked.

"Yes. That is our desire, to make it into the Kingdom."

Tom then took their translation of the Bible and read the following verses:

> Now there was a man of the Pharisees, Nicodemus, a ruler of the Jews. This one came to Him in the night and said to him: "Rabbi, we know that you as a teacher have come from God; for no one can perform these signs that you perform unless God is with him." In answer, Jesus said to him: "Most truly I say to you, *Unless anyone is born again he cannot see the Kingdom of God.*"[2]

"So when have you been born again?" Tom asked.

The reaction was almost comical. First, the deer-in-the-headlights look; then a clearing of the throat followed by nervous coughing; then J.W. looked at the trainee as if to say, "Don't just sit there, say something," while the trainee looked at J.W. the same way.

J.W. tried to change the subject, but Tom had a bulldog bite on his posterior (another apt metaphor) and was not about to let him go.

"So when have you been born again?"

Waving the white flag, J.W. abruptly ended the conversation with a request to come back at a later time.

Tom thought this would be the end of it, but just a few days later,

J.W. returned, this time with *his* former trainer in tow. Feeling more feisty, J.W. started in again.

But Tom interrupted and said, "So when have you been born again?"

J.W.'s colleague (we'll call him J.W.T.) had obviously prepped him for this question. J.W. said, "When I met J.W.T., he showed me how I needed to be baptized into his religion and keep God's commandments. Ever since, I have been born again."

"That's not what it means to be born again," Tom said.

The smug look on both their faces disappeared quicker than a chicken leg at an alligator ranch.

"You say you know the Scriptures," Tom said. "Show me where the Bible says baptism and obedience are the keys to being born again."

J.W. gave that same look to J.W.T. he had given his trainee—and got the same one back. Then for the first time, J.W. asked a question: "So, what does it mean to be born again?"

Of all the questions this book is attempting to answer, this may be the greatest one of all. For if what Jesus said is true, if we get this answer wrong, none of the other questions really matter.

If heaven exists, then it's critical to ask, "Can I get there from here? If I can, how do I get there? And can I know for sure that I'm going there?"

Let's go deeper. What if this life is just a journey to get us ready for real life? What if real life is far more than a physical life in a temporary physical world but a spiritual life in an eternal spiritual world? Jesus Himself said to people who thought they were experiencing real life and all it had to offer, "I have come that they might have life, and have it to the full."[3]

Jesus was talking about a different kind of life—a life that is found in what the Bible calls being born again. If true life can be found only in a relationship with God through a new birth, then there is not a more important topic for us to consider. I have found that people who have never experienced this new birth have one of three problems:

1. They don't understand what being born again is.
2. They don't believe what it is.
3. They won't accept what it is.

A man by the name of Nicodemus came to Jesus with all three problems. The Gospel of John records what may be the most important one-on-one conversation Jesus ever had, and it is during this conversation that we are introduced to the concept of being "born again."

As with a lot of other things we have succeeded in dumbing down, the term *born again* is used to describe everything from an athlete who makes a comeback to a company that rises from the ashes of bankruptcy. The term *born again* probably needs to be born again.

Even among churchgoers you will often hear the expression "born-again Christian," which is a redundancy, a kind of theological stuttering. If you are born again, you are a Christian. If you are a Christian, you are born again. There is no such thing as a nonborn-again Christian, nor is there any such thing as a born-again non-Christian.[4]

It is extremely important that we understand exactly what that phrase means, for according to Jesus, our eternal destiny hangs on it. Jesus states unequivocally that only those who are "born again" will even see, much less enter, the Kingdom of God.

Jesus said something to Nicodemus that shook him from head to toe and shattered everything he had ever been taught and believed. It will rock the world of many modern-day Nicodemuses who follow the majority view that good people go to heaven. In effect Jesus said, "You don't have to be a member of the church, you don't have to be baptized, you don't have to be religious, and you don't have to do good works to go to heaven. The one thing that must be true of you if you are going to heaven is you must be born again."

Amazingly, we are going to learn that *real life begins with a second birthday.*

As we study this fascinating encounter between one of the most respected Old Testament scholars of his day and an uneducated carpenter from Nazareth, we learn what we need to do in order to be born again.

## Conceive It—Get It into Your Mind

The protagonist in this fascinating encounter is Nicodemus. John takes pains to inform us exactly who Jesus is dealing with: "Now there was a Pharisee, a man named Nicodemus who was a member of the Jewish ruling council."[5]

Nicodemus was a Pharisee, which meant he was one of about six thousand in that religious sect. Jews considered Pharisees the spiritual crème de la crème, the religious elite revered by the masses. More than anyone else, they made sure to dot every religious *i* and cross every *t*. A Pharisee never missed going to synagogue. He gave a tithe of his income every week. He was as morally straight as a Boy Scout and as theologically straight as a gun barrel. If anyone was thought to have a lock on heaven, it was the Pharisees. They weren't just considered morally good but morally *superior.*

Furthermore, Nicodemus was a "member of the Jewish ruling council." This was otherwise known as the Sanhedrin—the Jewish Supreme Court, Parliament, and Vatican rolled into one.[6] It had only seventy members, and they ruled over the Jewish nation.

He had risen through the ranks until he had become the most respected of all his peers. Jesus called him "Israel's teacher"[7]—the greatest religious authority of all the Pharisees, the dean of the Devoted

Department. He would have been voted "most likely to make it to heaven because God couldn't turn down such a great guy."

---

> Jesus was more than a great teacher; He was
> a miracle worker and was even running
> around dispensing forgiveness.

---

But a new kid had come to town who was taking the masses by storm. He was teaching spiritual truth so liberating in comparison to the stifling pharisaical legalism so long in vogue that everywhere He went, it was standing room only. The more people heard *about* Him, the more they wanted to hear *from* Him.

But Jesus was more than a great teacher; He was a miracle worker and was even running around dispensing forgiveness. And that got Nicodemus's attention since *forgiveness is a God thing.* But what really got Nick's attention was that people were beginning to mention the M word—*Messiah.*

Nicodemus had heard one side of the story from his buddies, who were convinced that Jesus was a dangerous interloper who would upset their applecart. Not only that, the Roman government frowned on anyone who gathered too great a following. Nicodemus wanted to size up the competition firsthand. *I've got to meet this guy myself,* he determined.

> He came to Jesus at night and said, "Rabbi, we know that
> you are a teacher who has come from God. For no one
> could perform the signs you are doing if God were not
> with him."[8]

Knowing that Jesus didn't always get along with the Pharisees, Nicodemus goes to Him in private and says exactly what most of the world says today about Jesus. It's what every religion outside of Christianity says. It's even what most nonreligious people say about Jesus: "Oh yes—good fellow, great teacher, and brilliant mind." Nicodemus commends Jesus as someone who has come from God and knows what He's talking about.

John clues us in that something else is going on with Nicodemus when he adds the little detail about him coming at night. John's Gospel mentions only two people who came to Jesus at night: Nicodemus and Judas. Both men had one thing in common—they were living in spiritual darkness. Nicodemus came to Jesus at night, and what he needed was to see the light.

> Nicodemus was confronted with this shattering thought—good isn't good enough. Your works won't work. If you're going to get into the Kingdom of God and spend eternity with the God of the Kingdom, you must be born again.

Regardless, at this point, Nicodemus is probably waiting on Jesus to return the compliment—telling him what a great scholar he is or how He has heard about his theological brilliance. Maybe he thought they would talk philosophy or have a nice friendly debate on some scriptural passages they disagreed on…and then Jesus brings up something about birthdays.

> Jesus replied, "Very truly I tell you, no one can see the kingdom of God unless they are born again."[9]

Jesus gets right to the heart of the matter. He says, "Nicodemus, you think the way to God is through religion, good works, keeping the law, doing your best, or a combination of all these things. You don't understand that it has nothing to do with doing, but it has everything to do with becoming and being."

For the first time in his life, Nicodemus was confronted with this shattering thought—good isn't good enough. Your best won't do. Your works won't work. If you're going to get into the Kingdom of God and spend eternity with the God of the Kingdom, you must be born again.

There's another reason Jesus uses this birth analogy. Nicodemus had no problem with a birth being the way to God, but he had been taught and was teaching that being a citizen of God's Kingdom was a matter of *physical birth*. He believed that being born a descendant of Abraham automatically made you a Kingdom citizen. You might say that for a Jew, a relationship with God was a matter of "in and out"—you were *in* the Kingdom the moment you were *out* of your mother's womb.

What about those who were not born Jewish? The answer was simple: Convert to Judaism. This involved a period of instruction in the Jewish law, baptism as a ceremonial form of washing, and for men— well, let's just say it involved some *very* delicate surgery. Only then could a non-Jew be considered a child of Abraham (though somewhat adopted) and thus a card-carrying Kingdom citizen.

Had Jesus left out the word *again* after the word *born*, Nick would have gone his merry way. Obviously a person must be born to get into *any* kingdom. If Jesus had said "born Jewish" or "born to Jewish parents," Nicodemus would have gone back and given a big thumbs-up to his Pharisee buddies and assured them Jesus was A-OK. But no... Kingdom entrance was granted only through a passport stamped "born again" on the front.

Talk about the ultimate myth buster. According to Jesus, Kingdom citizenship depends on one thing: *How many birthdays have you had?* We all get one. Jesus said the second birthday is even more important than the first. The first is for time and the second is for eternity. The first is for earth and the second is for heaven.

Jesus said Kingdom entrance is not a matter of personal reformation, cleaning up your act, turning over a new leaf, trying to do better, or getting religion. It's all about a birth—a *spiritual* birth.

Nicodemus didn't understand that being born into a Jewish family (or a Christian family) doesn't make you a child of God any more than being born in a garage makes you a car. It wouldn't matter if Billy Graham were your father and Joan of Arc your mother. God only has children, not grandchildren. Kingdom citizenship has nothing to do with your physical birth, but it has everything to do with your spiritual birth.

The word translated "again" is the Greek word *anothen*, which can also mean "above."[10] A physical birth from below won't cut it—one must experience a spiritual birth from above. The first birth gets you on the earth; the second birth prepares you for eternity.

Let's give Nicodemus some credit. Today try telling people they must be born again, and with either sincere incredulity or self-righteous arrogance, they will ask "Why?" Jesus struck a chord in Nick's heart. He knew that Jesus was on to something, so he didn't ask "Why?" He asked "How?" He had taken the first step toward being born again by seeking to understand what it means. For someone to experience the new birth, it's vital they understand both its necessity as well as its nature. Nick was on the road to taking the second step.

## Receive It—Open Your Heart to the Truth

Nicodemus could have thrown up his hands, walked away, and joined the ranks of the skeptics and critics. In a way, who could blame him as he had just been told that both his Jewish pedigree and educational degree were spiritually worthless. But the iron of his heart could not escape the magnetic force of this amazing man and this before unheard-of teaching. The scholar had become the seeker.

"How can someone be born when they are old?" Nicodemus asked. "Surely they cannot enter a second time into their mother's womb to be born!"[11]

He knew that was impossible. He realized that Jesus was talking symbolically. Nicodemus knew deep in his heart that in spite of all his religion and righteousness, he was one flawed, imperfect human being, sinful just like everybody else. What he was saying was, "I wish I could put my life in reverse. I wish I could rewind the tape. I wish I got a do-over. I wish I could get a new start, but how can this happen? Nobody can start over. Nobody can erase the past…or can they?"

So many people treat their spiritual lives as a do-it-yourself project. Go to a home improvement store, get the necessary tools, and build your own ramp to God through religion, ritual, and self-righteousness. But all self-built ramps not only fall short, they actually lead us farther away from God. Like Nicodemus, we must receive what God wants to do for us rather than continue to offer what we can do for Him. Nick was beginning to realize this and was only one step away from a brand-new spiritual birth.

## Believe It—Experience the Transformation in Your Life

Nicodemus closes his part of the conversation with a question: "How can this be?"[12] He is now disturbed and desperate. Everything he had been taught and everything he thought has been challenged and contradicted. Being born a Jew, being religious, going to the synagogue, observing the law, doing good works—none of these things get one foot into the Kingdom. He is asking the most important question: "How can I be born again?"

Jesus first pinpoints his problem and then points out the solution. First the problem:

"Very truly I tell you, we speak of what we know, and we testify to what we have seen, but still you people do not accept our testimony. I have spoken to you of earthly things and you do not believe; how then will you believe if I speak of heavenly things?"[13]

Nicodemus's real problem was unbelief. "You do not accept" and "you do not believe" mean the same thing. Understand that when Jesus met Nicodemus it was not just an encounter between two religious people; it was a collision between two philosophies and two opposing views.

Nicodemus thought you have to work to be accepted by God. But Jesus told this Jewish scholar, child of Abraham, Eagle Scout, altar boy, son of a preacher man, "You don't need a new start; you need a new life, and it's a new life that only God can give you." It was a life-changing, mind-altering revelation, and the light was beginning to come on for this man who had lived in darkness all his life without realizing it.

Everyone on earth got here by birth, but not one person chose to be born. You didn't choose where you were born. You didn't choose when you were born. You didn't choose what family you were born into. Physical birth happened to you without any effort whatsoever on your part. The same thing is true of spiritual birth. You were born because God chose to give you life, and you are born again because God chooses to give you spiritual life.

Jesus is relentless in His pursuit of His fellow Jew's heart: "You should not be surprised at my saying, 'You must be born again.'"[14]

The look of amazement on Nick's face gave him away. It's the same look I have seen from people who never attend church to those who never miss church when they are confronted with this truth: *Being born again is not making a new start in life; it is receiving a new life to start with.*

---

When it comes to the new birth,
Jesus said God does all the work.

---

A certain retired man always scanned the obituary column first when he read the newspaper. One morning, much to his amazement and consternation, he found his name included on the list. He called the newspaper editor and chewed him out. "What are you going to do about this colossal blunder?" he said. The editor thought for a moment and said, "Sir, I've got a great idea. In the morning, we'll put your name in the birth announcements and give you a brand-new start."

A brand-new start is what God provides in the new birth. It has nothing to do with anything we do for God; it has everything to do with what God does in us, through us, and for us. There is no such thing as a do-it-yourself new birth.

When it comes to the new birth, Jesus said God does all the work. Nicodemus thought he had to earn Kingdom entrance. Jesus said it was a gift. Nicodemus thought his salvation was a trade-off—physical birth plus self-righteousness in exchange for a Kingdom passport. But Jesus said it's something you receive when you believe.

Then Jesus added the kicker: "No one has ever gone into heaven except the one who came from heaven—the Son of Man."[15]

Wow! Jesus has just upped the ante big-time. Jesus was not just claiming to be "sent from God"—the claim of a prophet. He was asserting that He had come from heaven—the claim of divinity. Nicodemus's mind must have been spinning faster than a rocket-powered carousel. Either this man is a complete nut job, or He is the Messiah Nicodemus has been hoping for.

To drive the point home, John records what is universally acclaimed as the greatest verse in the Bible:

"For God so loved the world that he gave his one and only Son, that whoever believes in him shall not perish but have eternal life."[16]

Nicodemus had never heard this before. Entrance into God's Kingdom, acceptance into God's family is not a matter of following rules, getting into a system, or performing some ritual. It is "everyone who believes may have eternal life in him."[17] The Kingdom does not come to the one who achieves but to the one who believes. Nicodemus must have staggered as if he had been hit with a right hook from Mohammed Ali. Eternal life is received by trusting not trying. No law keeping, religion abiding, or rule obeying enters into the equation. It's as simple as 2 + 2 = 4; trusting = eternal life.

---

Jesus was offering the simplest of routes
to God's acceptance—faith.

---

And if that's true, everybody has equal access—Jews, Gentiles, skeptics, hypocrites…the list goes on. In contrast to the meticulous rule-keeping system of Nicodemus's pharisaical lifestyle,[18] Jesus was offering the simplest of routes to God's acceptance—faith.

But please note, Jesus was not speaking of simple intellectual assent to some truth but of a complete surrender of the heart. True belief results in a confession of sin and surrender to this Son sent into the world to die for all sin. True belief moves one to totally abandon any idea of a self-made, self-achieved salvation. True belief is nothing short of complete trust in Jesus as the only source of eternal life.

It is not coincidental that Jesus spoke of being born again with one of the most respected, religious, and righteous (at least outwardly) men in the New Testament. How appropriate that Jesus told this man he had to be born again so that everyone would know that all must be born again, from the religious to the rebellious and from the righteous to the reprobate.

Now we know beyond a shadow of a doubt why Jesus came. *Jesus Christ was born physically that we might be born again spiritually.* He left heaven as the Son of God and came to earth as the Son of Man so that sons and daughters of men might leave this earth and go to heaven as sons and daughters of God. And the only way that transformation takes place is through the new birth.

---

According to Jesus, no one is "just born a Christian."
There must be a point in time when you are born
again spiritually, just as there was a day
when you were born physically.

---

I painfully include a story that illustrates how vital it is to take the words of Jesus seriously. Former president George W. Bush recounts the time in 1985 when the entire Bush family had gathered in Kennebunkport, Maine, for their annual family reunion. Billy Graham had been invited to join them, and after dinner they gathered around Dr. Graham for questions. Bush picks up the story:

> The first question was from Dad. He said, "Billy, some people say you have to have a born-again experience to go to heaven. Mother [my grandmother] here is the most religious, kind person I know, yet she has had no born-again experience. Will she go to heaven?" Wow, pretty profound question from the old man. We all looked at Billy. In his quiet, strong voice, he replied, "George, some of us require a born-again experience to understand God, and some of us are born Christians. It sounds as if your mom was just born a Christian."[19]

Make no mistake. According to Jesus, no one is "just born a Christian." Jesus made it plain that there must be a point in time when you are born again spiritually, just as there was a day when you were born physically. According to Jesus, the answer to one simple question can tell you whether your passport has been stamped for God's Kingdom: "How many times have you been born?" If you have been born only once, you are going to die twice. You are going to die physically, and then you are going to die spiritually. But if you have been born twice, you are going to die only once. So, "How many times have you been born?"

You were born for one purpose—to be born again. Contrary to what they teach you in Harvard Business School, you need to do only one thing before you leave this planet. You don't have to succeed. You don't have to grow up. You don't have to get married. You don't have to have children. You don't have to make money. You don't have to get an education. You don't have to buy a home or a car. You don't have to live to retirement.

But if you want to see and enter God's Kingdom, you must be born again.

CHAPTER TEN

# Are People of Other Faiths with You in Heaven or Only Jesus-Followers?

In every chapter thus far, I have shared with you a personal encounter I have had with someone who had a question for God or about God. I'm going to make an exception in this chapter. Though I've never met this person, in some ways I feel I have.

Fame? She may be the most famous female on this planet. She is one of the few people universally known by her first name. (I could give you the first letter of her first name and you would most likely know who I'm talking about.) Her notoriety has been achieved through hosting the highest-rated talk show in history,[1] and she became the youngest person to receive the International Radio and Television Society's "Broadcaster of the Year" award.[2] Her face is one of the most recognized anywhere.

Fortune? *Forbes* magazine disclosed in 2003 that she was the first African-American woman to become a billionaire, and from 2004–2006, listed her as the world's only black billionaire on the planet.[3] She was declared as the richest African-American of the twentieth century and although black people are 13 percent of the U.S. population,[4] she has remained the only black American to rank among America's four hundred richest people every year since 1995.[5] Her net worth as of September 2010 was $2.7 billion, and she is the highest paid TV entertainer in the United States, receiving an annual income of almost $300 million.[6]

Still, what is most impressive about this media giant is her global influence. CNN and Time.com called her "arguably the world's most powerful woman."[7] Another prominent publication called her "the most influential woman in the world."[8] *Time* named her "one of the most influential people" from 2004–2010, the only person to have appeared on the list each of those years.[9] In 2010, *Life* named her one of the 100 people who changed the world, alongside such notables as Jesus Christ and Elvis Presley. She was the only living woman to make that list.[10] By one estimate, her support of Barack Obama delivered over a million votes in the 2008 Democratic primary giving him the nomination.[11]

Unless you've been in a Rip Van Winkle coma since the Carter administration, you know I'm talking about the one and only Oprah Winfrey. When Oprah talks, untold millions listen, so much so that her ability to influence both public opinion and consumer preferences has been dubbed "the Oprah effect."[12] As an example, the Oprah Book Club segment on her television show has meant instant bestseller status and up to a million additional sales for the authors she selected.[13]

In the spiritual realm, Oprah has become for many almost a papal authority with her congregation dubbed "The Church of O."[14] She is a twenty-first century high priestess of sorts to her congregation of more than twenty-two million.[15] So contemplate this priestly pronouncement from the Right Reverend Oprah: "One of the biggest mistakes we make is to believe there is only one way [to God]. There are many diverse paths leading to God."[16]

> Among Americans, 75 percent believe that many religions lead to eternal life, and nearly 50 percent of the most strongly committed, white evangelical Protestants do not hold to their faith as the only path to salvation.

Now before we defrock Reverend Winfrey, let us admit that she states the belief held overwhelmingly in a variety of circles today. Bill Bradley, former U.S. senator, NBA star with the New York Knicks, and active in the Fellowship of Christian Athletes, once said in a gospel tract titled "I've Made My Choice," published in the 1960s, "I've made my choice. I love Jesus Christ and I try to serve Him to the best of my ability. How about you?"

But Bradley, an erstwhile contender for the Democratic presidential nomination, peddled backward at warp speed in his autobiography *Time Present, Time Past*:

> Christianity offers one way to achieve it [inner peace, a oneness with themselves and the world]; Buddhism, Judaism, Islam, Confucianism, Hinduism, offer others…Increasingly, I resist the exclusivity of "true believers." Isn't it better to remain open, so that you may learn from another's truth…I choose my own individual faith.[17]

That view is now the prevalent view in the most Christian-oriented nation on the planet. Nearly two-thirds of Americans consider religion to be *important* in their lives, and 60 percent see religious faith as essential to a strong America. Yet a full 75 percent believe that many religions lead to eternal life, and nearly 50 percent of the most strongly committed, white evangelical Protestants do not hold to their faith as the only path to salvation.[18]

The view that every other faith is wrong except Christianity is met with disdain and even alarm. Charles Templeton bloviates against the unbelievable arrogance of anyone who holds to a narrow evangelical view of salvation:

> Christians are a small minority in the world. Approximately four out of five people on the face of the earth believe in gods other than the Christian God. The more than five billion people who live on earth revere or worship more than three hundred gods. If one includes the animist or tribal religions, the number rises to more than three thousand. *Are we to believe that only Christians are right?*[19]

Some even consider a belief in the uniqueness of any faith or truth claim a red-alert danger to world peace. One American theologian avers:

> I have come to believe that this exclusivist tendency in my own faith tradition—and in other traditions—is a serious barrier to genuine peace-making in a world of religious pluralism. For Christianity, the claim that salvation is possible only in Jesus Christ is, in the end, dismissive of other religious traditions and inherently divisive. If Christians are to be instruments of the peace of God, we must develop a new Christian theology of religions that will enable us to see God's revelation in Jesus Christ *while at the same time rejecting any claim to exclusivism.*[20]

In a day when the cream of the buzzword *tolerance* rises to the top of the milk of political correctness that most everyone is drinking, how do we respond to a seemingly logical call for spiritual humility? We are compelled to respond in light of the fact that Jesus Himself said it was possible for people to go to heaven—but not everyone would get there.

Erwin Lutzer points out three possible ways to respond to this call for abandoning any singular claim to religious truth and particularly the Christian emphasis on the uniqueness of Jesus Christ as the only way to God.[21]

The first response is *pluralism.* This perspective affirms the equality of all religions in their ability to connect with God.[22] No one religion, faith, or spiritual tradition is superior to any other. All have an equal place at the table of metaphysical, supernatural truth.

The second response is *inclusivism.* This approach is slightly more accommodating to Christianity in that it recognizes some uniqueness in Jesus, and perhaps even a measure of divinity, but it denies that He alone is the truth or that He is the only way to God. God may have revealed Himself through Jesus and the Bible, but no more than He did through Muhammad, Confucius, or some other spiritual figure or book.

> The predominant worldview is that there are many ways to get to heaven, and no one way is better than another...85 percent of Americans said they believed in heaven, and of those, more than 87 percent believed they were likely to go to heaven.

The third response is *exclusivism.* This view holds that God uniquely, specifically, and singularly revealed Himself only in and through Christ, and propositionally only in the Bible.[23] Therefore, the corollary truth must be that *all other religions are false.* Therein lies the rub.

The question we must answer is: Which of these three responses is called for by the claims of Christ and the Word of God?

In one of the most important conversations Jesus ever had with His disciples, He talked about life after death, and heaven in particular:

> "My Father's house has many rooms; if that were not so, would I have told you that I am going there to prepare a place for you? And if I go and prepare a place for you, I will come back and take you to be with me that you also may be where I am."[24]

Heaven is a prepared place for a specially prepared people, according to Jesus. Contrarily, the predominant worldview of the twenty-first century is that there are many ways to get to heaven, and no one way is better than another.

Interestingly enough, most people who believe in heaven believe they are going there. In a recent poll by *Fox News*, 85 percent of Americans said they believed in heaven, and of those, more than 87 percent believed they were likely to go to heaven. Only 13 percent thought they might not make it.[25]

When I read survey results like these, I'm reminded of the teacher lecturing her kids on spelling. She told the class she wanted each one of them to tell what their father did for a living and then spell his occupation. A girl named Mary went first. "My dad is a baker. B-A-K-E-R. If he were here, he would give everyone a cookie."

Next came Tommy. "My dad is a banker. B-A-N-K-E-R. If he were here, he would give everybody a dollar."

The third kid was Jimmy. He said, "My dad is an electrician." He tried several times to spell the word, but he just couldn't do it. Finally, the teacher asked him to sit down and think about it while she called on somebody else.

She turned to Johnny, and he said, "My dad is a bookie. B-O-O-K-I-E. If he were here, he would lay you 8 to 5 that Jimmy ain't never gonna spell *electrician*."

Odds are that a lot of people who think they're going to heaven are not because they don't know the three things that are essential for anyone to go there. First, they must believe in heaven. Second, they have to want to go to heaven. Third and most important, *they have to know the way to heaven.*

After Jesus told His disciples that He was going to heaven and would prepare a place for them there so they could spend eternity with Him, Thomas asked Him, "Lord, we don't know where you are going, so how can we know the way?"[26]

Jesus did not just give an answer; He dropped a bomb. He gave the "Nuclear Option." He gave the mother of all politically incorrect statements. He made a claim that, if true, means that *every other religion in the world is dead wrong.*

It is not unusual for Jesus to make statements that turn conventional thinking on its head. He often shocked people with teachings that cut across the grain of human nature and were diametrically opposed to what most people thought. For example, He said such things as:

"The way to save your life is to lose it."

"The first will be last and the last will be first."

"Rejoice when you are persecuted."

"Pray for your enemies."

"Turn the other cheek."

"It is better to give than to receive."

Still, the most outrageous, in-your-face statement Jesus ever made is the one that did as much as anything to get Him crucified: "I am the way and the truth and the life. No one comes to the Father except through me."[27]

If Dale Carnegie were alive today, he would say to Jesus, "That is *not* the way to win friends and influence people." If political incorrectness were explosive, this statement could end the universe as we know it. However, Jesus Christ must be judged, evaluated, and considered by this statement more than any other He made.

---

One of the threads that runs through every other religion in the world is that sincerity of religious belief or participation in religious activity is the way to God.

---

Why would I make such a claim? If that statement is true, it is the most important truth you will ever be told, and it must be true for everyone. If it is false, it is the biggest lie you will ever be told, and it must be false for everyone. Since Jesus is the only person ever to have made such an audacious, breathtaking claim, it behooves every person to decide its veracity and its implications.

Admittedly, any claim from Jesus has validity only if (a) He was who He said He was—the Son of God, and (b) He did what He said He did—died for the sins of the world and came back from the grave. I freely concede that if either (a) or (b) is not true, all bets are off. But assuming for the moment both propositions are true, then the implications for every other religion and spiritual movement are absolutely staggering. This statement is the ultimate myth buster.

According to Jesus, two common beliefs held in some form or fashion by almost the entire non-Christian world (and even some within that world) are absolutely false.

## False Belief One: *I Can Rely on Religion to Get to God*

One of the threads that runs through every other religion in the world is that sincerity of religious belief or participation in religious activity is the way to God. This is one of the two worldviews that dominate twenty-first century thinking about heaven and how to get there.

Bill O'Reilly of *The O'Reilly Factor* summed up this thinking perfectly by telling this joke:

> Saint Peter was leading a group of new arrivals on their first tour of heaven. Suddenly he stopped and put his finger to his mouth. "Shhh," he whispered. "We can't make a sound when we walk by this room. Remember that." When they passed out of hearing range, one of the new souls asked, "Why?" Peter replied, "Because that room is full of Southern Baptists and they think they are the only ones up here."

Funny joke, but then listen to what O'Reilly says next:

> I found that any remark I make about religion is likely to make some viewers steaming mad, and the fundamentalists really hate it when I say something like this: the most important thing I can say about religion is that it is a good thing for all of us to have. It doesn't matter what you believe—as long as you believe in *something*.[28]

Mr. O'Reilly unwittingly exposes the first myth that all religions are basically the same and teach fundamentally the same thing. Each may be a different road to God and may take a different turn or twist here and there, but they all lead to the same place.

---

If the only path to God is through Jesus Christ,
then Christianity cannot be reconciled
with any other religion.

---

We know this belief cannot be true, because with Jesus' one statement about His uniqueness, He put Christianity in a class by itself. If the only path to God is through Jesus Christ, then Christianity cannot be reconciled with any other religion.

To be clear, the uniqueness of Christianity is grounded in the uniqueness of Jesus Christ Himself. Other religious leaders say, "Follow me and I will show you the way to salvation," but Jesus said, "*I am the way* to salvation." Other religious leaders say, "Follow me and I'll show you how to find the truth," but Jesus said, "*I am the truth*." Other religious leaders say, "Follow me and I'll show you how you can live a meaningful life," but Jesus said, "*I am the life*."

Jesus said in effect that religion, either its presence or absence, has no bearing on one's relationship to God. Even more amazing is that Jesus put *Himself*, not the religion He established, up against all others.

Beyond that, if religion—any religion—is sufficient to establish a link to the Almighty, then there is no explanation for Jesus' birth, life, or death. It is not too great a stretch to assert that the fact that Jesus came, lived, and died *necessitates* His dogmatic statement to be the only way to God. If God went to the extreme of sending His own Son as the universal sacrifice for sin, providing His birth through a virgin and raising Him bodily from the dead, the audacity does not lie with Jesus but with any other religious leader or system that would challenge His claim.

So the answer to the question, "How do you know Christianity is true and all other religions are false?" is relatively simple. If Jesus Christ was who He said He was and did what He said He did, thereby making Christianity true, then at every point at which any other religion contradicts Christianity, that religion must be false.

If you have not personally placed your trust in Jesus Christ, it doesn't matter how religious you are. It's not that religion is bad—it's that it is worthless for connecting with God.

But for many, this myth buster poses no problem. Hundreds of millions of people who have no use or interest in religion whatsoever are convinced they are nevertheless "in" with the divine. For them, Jesus' statement poses a different problem.

## False Belief Two: *I Can Rely on My Righteousness to Get to God*

The other predominant worldview of the twenty-first century is this: If there is a heaven, you earn your way there by good works and living a good life. I often ask people I engage in spiritual conversation, "If God appeared to you and asked, 'Why should I let you into heaven?' how would you answer that question?" The vast majority of the answers begin along these lines:

"I've always tried to…"

"I have never…"

"I've tried to do my very best…"

It doesn't matter if I'm talking to a religious person or nonreligious person, the answer usually goes back to that person's attempt to live a good life. Why is that? Because the other predominant worldview is that good people go to heaven.

---

> If you try to build a highway to heaven with your own good works, you're building a toll road. You have to pay your own way as you go along, and you will run out of road long before you get to your destination.

---

Jim Dwyer, who played professional baseball with the Baltimore Orioles, was asked if he thought Pete Rose should be allowed into the Hall of Fame. He said, "Yes. The Hall of Fame is for baseball people. Heaven is for good people."[29]

To most people, salvation is kind of like going to Home Depot. (Frankly, when I go to Home Depot, I'm only tagging along with

Teresa because she's the fix-it person in our household.) People who go to Home Depot are into do-it-yourself projects. If something needs to be done around their house, they want to do it themselves, build it themselves, or repair it themselves.

That's the way a lot of people try to form a relationship with God. "I can build my own highway to God. I can do this myself. I can be good enough. I can be nice enough. I can give enough. I can go to church enough. I can get this done without anybody's help. I can build my own highway to heaven."

That kind of thinking reminds me of a verse in Proverbs that says, "There is a way that seems right to a man, but its end is the way to death."[30]

The Home Depot way of getting to God has several problems. First, if you try to build a highway to heaven with your own good works, you're building a toll road. You have to pay your own way as you go along, and you will run out of road long before you get to your destination because *good is never good enough.*

Second, the road is actually a dead-end bypass. If you try to be good enough for God, you will wind up getting further from God rather than closer to Him because *mere human goodness bypasses the cross of Christ and the grace of God.*

Third, the road of human righteousness actually goes the wrong way. It denies the need for a sacrifice for sin and a Savior, and thus it takes one further from the God who provides both through His Son.

On the other hand, God's highway to heaven is a freeway. It's *free* and it's going the right *way.* It's not a toll road that you pay for through good deeds, charitable works, or human effort. It's a freeway that has already been built and paid for by God's Son, and it is accessible at all times to all people.

The Bible cannot make it any plainer than this: "God saved you by his grace when you believed. And you can't take credit for this; it is a gift from God. Salvation is not a reward for the good things we have done, so none of us can boast about it."[31]

---

Every other religion in the world spells salvation "d-o"; Christianity spells salvation "d-o-n-e."

---

Every other religion calls for some kind of self-effort, rule keeping, and ritual observance. Whether it's using a Tibetan prayer wheel, making a sacred pilgrimage, giving to the poor, avoiding particular foods, performing a number of good deeds, praying in a certain way, or going through a cycle of reincarnation, all religions come to the same place—*it all depends on me.*

Every other religion in the world spells salvation "d-o," because the way to God depends in some way on *what you do.* Christianity spells salvation "d-o-n-e," because *Jesus Christ has already done* what we need for salvation by His death on the cross.

When the disciples asked Jesus the way to heaven, He never mentions religion or righteousness. He never alludes to church or commandments. He refers to Himself. It's as if Jesus were saying, "The way to heaven? Hello! You've been looking at Him, talking to Him, and living with Him for the last three years." Jesus drives His point home with the force of a nuclear-powered sledgehammer, making plain how anyone can get to God.

## I Must Rely on a Relationship to Get to God

Look at the last part of this statement again: "No one comes to the Father except through me."[32]

With that one statement, Jesus struck a fatal blow to universalism, the doctrine that says that all roads lead to heaven, that one way is just as good as another and eventually everybody is going to wind up in the same place.

Against this incredibly narrow, exclusivist statement, every other religion in the world joins forces to demand "Why? Why would Jesus say that, and how can it possibly be true?" The formulation of the answer begins at the beginning of time recorded in the opening chapters of the Bible. It started when the first human being said something to God never uttered before by anyone other than Satan himself.[33] Adam said "no" to a specific command from God. And at that moment, sin entered into the world.

A spiritual barrier was erected instantaneously between humanity and God that is impervious to human efforts to tear it down. It is a bridge too far, a chasm too wide, an ocean too deep to be crossed by human effort alone. From that moment, the greatest need of the human race was to be reconciled with God. That reconciliation is possible only if that sin is dealt with to God's satisfaction.

God is the offended party, and God alone has the authority to set the terms for that reconciliation to take place. It truly is "God's way or the highway," and God's way is through an atoning sacrifice for sin. God is too holy and righteous to allow any sin to be overlooked. Sin requires a sinless sacrifice,[34] and God provided that sacrifice through Jesus Christ, who lived a sinless life and paid the price for every sin committed past, present, and future. His resurrection proved that He was who He said He was and He did what He said He did, and it gave Him the right to make this narrow, exclusive, dogmatic but true statement.[35]

The story of Christ in toto presents the biggest challenge for those who wish to dismiss Jesus' claim to be the only way to God. If there is any other way to God except through Jesus Christ, then why did Jesus come and die? What kind of God would allow His Son to die such a horrible, ignominious death, bearing the sins of the world, if it was all unnecessary? If all roads lead to the same place, if one can build his own bridge to God by religious adherence, righteous deeds, ritualistic observance, or a combination thereof, the cross was either the blunder of the ages or the sick act of a sadistic God who doesn't deserve our worship, for no father would *unnecessarily* sacrifice his son for anyone or any cause.

---

> You can have religion without Jesus,
> but you can't have Christianity without Christ.

---

Louis Marcos in his excellent book *Apologetics in the 21st Century* puts the matter succinctly but strongly:

> God did not send his son to earth to die a painful death to provide us with an "option"; he did it because the incarnation (Christmas), the atonement (Good Friday), and the Resurrection (Easter) offered the *only possible remedy* to the problem of original sin.[36]

Unlike any other religious leader who has ever lived, Jesus Christ authenticated who He was by what He did. He lived a perfect life. He fulfilled scores of prophecies made centuries before He was even born. He performed miracles. He healed the sick and raised the dead. And He offered up Himself on the cross as the perfect sacrifice for sins and, in the ultimate coup de grâce, fulfilled His own prophecy by being raised from the dead. When the Jesus of the New Testament is honestly evaluated, He *alone* of all the spiritual figures in history has the right to make this unparalleled claim.

Perhaps it is dawning on you why Christianity and religion are so different. You can have religion without Jesus, but you can't have Christianity without Christ. You can be a Buddhist without knowing

Buddha. You can be a Muslim without knowing Muhammad. You can be a Confucian without knowing Confucius. But you cannot be a Christian without personally knowing Jesus Christ.

I make no apology when I say to you that Jesus Christ is not just one of many ways to God. He is not just a good way to God. He is not a relatively better way to God. He is not even the best of all ways to God. He is the *only* way to God. A Bethlehem manger, a Jerusalem cross, and an empty tomb all bear witness to the uniqueness of Christ and the singularity of His salvation.

---

If there is any way to God other than Jesus Christ,
then you can only conclude that
Jesus Christ is a liar, a fake, and a fraud.

---

A group of hikers gathered for a trek in the Canadian wilderness. The hikers had paid a premium for this rugged test. They arrived at the camp early in the morning and spent several hours preparing packs, supplies, and food for the long journey ahead. But as they were preparing to leave, one of the more experienced hikers noticed to his dismay that the guide lacked maps for the backcountry they were about to explore. He inquired further and discovered the guide didn't even have a compass. The hiker informed several of his friends, and they anxiously confronted the guide about his lack of preparation for such a dangerous journey.

After listening to their concern, the guide, with the bright light of supreme confidence glowing on his face, replied, "Maps and compasses are not the way through these mountains; I am the way through these mountains."[37]

Jesus has thrown down the gauntlet. He said in no uncertain terms, "Neither religion nor righteousness are the way to God. I am the way to God." If there is any way to God other than Jesus Christ, then you can only conclude that Jesus Christ is a liar, a fake, and a fraud. His life and death have real meaning only if His exclusive claim is true.

The phone rang at 1:00 a.m. in the home of Leo Winters, a brilliant Chicago surgeon. It was the hospital telling him that a young boy had been tragically mangled in a car accident. Dr. Winters's hands were probably the only ones in the city skilled enough to save that boy's life.

He threw on his clothes, jumped into his car, and chose the quickest route to the hospital, which took him through a dangerous neighborhood. He came to a stoplight, and a man in a gray hat and a dirty flannel shirt opened the door, pulled him out of the driver's seat, and screamed, "Give me your car!"

The doctor tried to explain that he was on an emergency call, but the carjacker refused to listen. He threw the doctor out of the car and sped off. Dr. Winters wandered for more than forty-five minutes looking for a phone so he could call a taxi. When he finally got to the hospital, more than an hour had passed. He ran through the hospital doors, up the stairs, and to the nurse's station.

The nurse on duty looked at him, shook her head, and said, "Doctor, I'm sorry but you're too late. The boy died about thirty minutes ago. His father is in the chapel if you want to see him. He's awfully upset because he couldn't understand why you didn't come to help."

Dr. Winters walked hurriedly down the hallway and entered the chapel. Weeping at the altar was a man dressed in a dirty flannel shirt and gray hat. The boy's father looked up at the doctor in horror as he realized his tragic mistake.[38]

How many people have made the tragic mistake of taking the wrong path, making the wrong choice, choosing the wrong way to God, only to push away the only one who provides peace with God and the divine presence in one's life? Norman Geisler, one of the preeminent apologists for the Christian faith, said:

> At the midnight of human ignorance there are a lot of lights in the sky. Noontime, there's only one. And that's Jesus Christ, the light of the world. Based on the evidence for who he was, there really aren't any comparisons...So I cast my lot with him.[39]

After looking at all the options, I too have made my choice—and it was rather easy. I decided to cast my vote—and my eternal destiny—on the one who came back from the dead.

That is why this tenth question is perhaps the most important question of all. When life is over and we pass from the temporal to the eternal, we will all stand before the God who can answer all of our questions with the ease of an Einstein answering an elementary student's science question. But then we won't be asking Him a question; He will be asking us.

He will ask only one question. He won't care about anything we fretted and sweated over during our short stay on this planet. He won't ask about our finances, fame, or fortune. He won't inquire about our portfolios, positions, or possessions. His question will be extremely short and to the point, but it will be the most important question we will ever answer:

"What did you do with My Son Jesus?"

# Notes

## Introduction: The Questions that Claw at Us

1. I still have this fact from the 1964 *World Book Encyclopedia* my dad bought me.

2. Blaise Pascal in *Pensees* 149.

## Chapter 1: God, Is the Bible Really Your Word?

1. I got this idea from Carl F.H. Henry's magisterial work *God, Revelation and Authority* (Waco, TX: Word Books, 1979).

2. Chuck Colson and Nancy Pearcey, *How Now Shall We Live?* (Wheaton, IL: Tyndale House Publishers, 1999), 17.

3. Kirk Johnson, "Colorado Court Bars Execution Because Jurors Consulted Bible," *New York Times*, March 29, 2005.

4. John 17:17.

5. Psalm 138:2 ESV.

6. Genesis 2:9.

7. Revelation 22:2.

8. Genesis 3:22-24.

9. John 1:29.

10. www.slsoftware.com/study/html_outlines/Accuracy_Of_The_Bible.html.

11. John 17:17.

12. http://endtimepilgrim.org/columbus.htm.

13. Isaiah 40:22.

14. Literally in the Hebrew, "sphere."

15. Ecclesiastes 1:6 NASB.

16. Leviticus 15:13 NASB.

17. Leviticus 17:11.

18. www.eons.com/blogs/entry/1332824-How-Many-Bible-Prophecies-Did -Jesus-Fulfill-

19. Ezekiel 30:13b ESV.

20. John Adams, February 22, 1756, in a diary entry. L.H. Butterfield, ed,. *Diary and Autobiography of John Adams* (Cambridge, MA: Belknap Press of Harvard Press, 1961), vol. 3, p. 9.

21. Peter Kreeft, *Yes or No: Straight Answers to Tough Questions About Christianity* (San Francisco: Ignatius Press, 1991), 91.

22. As Stephen Prothero brilliantly points out in *God Is Not One* (New York: HarperOne, 2010).

23. Quoted in Daniel Fuller, "I Was Just Thinking," *Today's Christian*, September 1977.

## Chapter 2: I Don't Understand...How Can You Be One God in Three Persons?

1. Anton La Guardia, *War Without End* (New York: St. Martin's Press, 2001), 31.

2. Alistair E. McGrath, *Intellectuals Don't Need God* (Grand Rapids, MI: Zondervan, 1993), 150.

3. Norman Geisler and Ron Rhodes, *Conviction Without Compromise* (Eugene, OR: Harvest House Publishers, 2008), 33.

4. Many people don't know that even the word *Bible* is not found in the Bible. We must believe whatever Scripture teaches regardless of whether the term we use to describe it is found in Scripture. One theologian wisely put it this way: "If I believe everything the Bible says about topic X and use a term not found in the Bible to describe the full teaching of Scripture on that point, am I not being more truthful to the Word than someone who limits themselves to only biblical terms, but rejects some aspect of God's revelation?" (Geisler and Rhodes, *Conviction*, 42).

5. 2 Corinthians 13:14.

6. 1 Timothy 3:16 NASB.

7. Isaiah 55:8-9.

8. Isaiah 40:18.

9. This is not to say that the doctrine of the Trinity cannot be discussed in a meaningful way or that it is an absurdity. Apologist Robert Bowman clarifies this clearly and concisely: "To say that the Trinity cannot be understood likewise is imprecise or at least open to misinterpretation. Trinitarian theologians do not mean to imply that the Trinity is unintelligible nonsense. Rather, the point they are making is that the Trinity cannot be fully fathomed, or comprehended, by the finite mind of a man. There is a difference

between gaining a basically correct understanding of something and having a complete, comprehensive, all-embracing perfect understanding of it" (Cited by Kenneth Richard Samples, *Without a Doubt* [Grand Rapids, MI: Baker Books, 2004], 70).

10. The great Christian pietist A.W. Tozer rightly observed, "The doctrine of the Trinity…is truth for the heart. The fact that it cannot be satisfactorily explained, instead of being against it, is in its favor. Such a truth had to be revealed; no one could imagine it" (Ibid., 63).

11. Isaiah 45:5.

12. 1 Timothy 2:5.

13. Genesis 1:1.

14. Genesis 1:26.

15. Genesis 1:27.

16. Deuteronomy 6:4.

17. Charles R. Swindoll, *Growing Deep in the Christian Life* (Portland, OR: Multnomah Press, 1986), 104. The use of the word *echad* is especially important as there is another Hebrew word *yachid* for one meaning "a single, solitary, indivisible one." The word Moses used in Deuteronomy 6:4 describes a unity in plurality, not a unity in singularity. For example, Genesis 1:5, which describes the first day of creation, says, "And there was evening, and there was morning—the first day." The word is *echad* not *yachid*. There is a plurality within unity: the plurality of evening and morning are in unity one day. Likewise, Genesis 2:24 states, "That is why a man leaves his father and mother and is united to his wife, and they become one flesh." Two distinct personalities become literally one flesh, one union of two souls (D. James Kennedy, *Solving Bible Mysteries* [Nashville, TN: Thomas Nelson Publishers, 2000], 156).

18. The Jewish rabbi Daniel Lapin makes a fascinating observation concerning the Hebrew language in this regard. He states: "I personally find it intriguing that the original colonies numbered thirteen. Thirteen disparate colonies become one, forming the United (united of course means one) States. It turns out that the Hebrew word for "one," *echad*, is made up of three Hebrew letters possessing values of 1, 8, and 4 for a total of 13. This is one of the reasons a Jewish boy becomes at *one* with the people at the age of thirteen.

"Examining a one-dollar bill reveals an abundance of thirteens. There are thirteen letters in both the phrase ANNUIT COEPTIS, printed above the pyramid, and in the phrase E PLURIBUS UNUM, printed above the eagle. (The latter phrase, of course, means "From many, *one*.") There are thirteen layers of stone in the pyramid, thirteen stars arranged above the eagle's head, and thirteen stripes on the eagle's breast. There are thirteen arrows grasped in its left talons; among the olive twigs in its right talons are thirteen olives, although you will need a magnifying glass to see them. You will find no such symbolic occurrence of the number thirteen on the five-dollar bill, nor on the ten or twenty. Thirteen is not linked to five, ten or twenty. In Hebrew, thirteen actually means one" (Rabbi Daniel Lapin, *America's Real War* [Sisters, OR: Multnomah Publishers, 1999], 122).

19. See Matthew 28:19 and 3:16-17.

20. See for example 1 Corinthians 8:4,6.

21. Samples, *Without a Doubt*, 65.

22. Paul Copan, *That's Just Your Interpretation* (Grand Rapids, MI: Baker Books, 2001), 123.

23. John Blanchard, *Will the Real Jesus Please Stand Up?* (Durham, England: Evangelical Press, 1989), 146.

24. 1 Kings 8:60.

25. Philippians 2:9-11, emphasis added.

26. 2 Corinthians 3:17.

27. Matthew 27:46; John 17:1-26; 20:17.

28. Titus 2:13.

29. Acts 5:3-4.

30. Colossians 1:16.

31. Job 26:13 NLT.

32. Ephesians 1:3-4.

33. Ephesians 1:7-8a.

34. Titus 3:5.

35. John 3:5-6.

36. 1 Peter 1:1-2.

37. John 6:27; Ephesians 4:6; Colossians 1:2-3.

38. John 1:1,14; 5:17-18; 8:48-59; 10:25-30; 20:26-28; 2 Peter 1:1.

39. Genesis 1:2; John 14:26; Acts 13:2-4; 28:25; Romans 8:9-11; Ephesians 4:30.

40. Matthew 3:16-17; Acts 7:55-56.

41. Deuteronomy 6:4-5; Isaiah 45:5-6; Romans 3:30; 1 Timothy 2:5.

42. Copan, *That's Just Your Interpretation*, 73.

## Chapter 3: Did You Use Evolution to Create the Universe?

1. As my aforementioned college philosophy professor asked, "Why are we here instead of not here?"

2. Genesis 1:1.

3. CNN.com, 1-13-2005.

4. Genesis 2:24-25 NLT.

5. Quoted in *Moody Monthly*, March/April 1999, 29.

6. L.H. Matthews, "Introduction," Charles Darwin, *Origin of the Species* (London: J.N. Dent and Sons, Ltd., 1971) x-xi.

7. www.pathlights.com/ce_encyclopedia/Encyclopedia/01-evol1.htm.

8. Keep in mind I am referring to macroevolution that espouses life coming from nonlife and the phenomenon of one species evolving into another species.

9. Quoted in John M. Corbett, "In the Beginning, God," September 1, 2004, http://johncorbett.org/didyouknow.aspx.

10. www.jesus-is-savior.com/Evolution%20Hoax/wheres_the_proof_of_evolu tion.htm.

11. Duane Gish, "In the Beginning God—Or Hydrogen," *Christianity Today*, October 8, 1992, 32.

12. Richard Dawkins, *The Blind Watchmaker* (New York: Norton, 1986), 287. Emphasis in the original.

13. www.myfortress.org/evolution.htmf.

14. *World*, February 26, 2000, 32.

15. Philip E. Johnson, *Darwin on Trial*, 2nd ed. (Downers Grove, IL: InterVarsity Press, 1993), 26-27.

16. "Mutations are simply errors in DNA replication," according to University of Chicago biologist Jerry Coyne. "The chance of a mutation happening is indifferent to whether it would be helpful or harmful." Harmful mutations mean fewer offspring to the organism carrying it and more offspring for helpful mutations—hence "natural selection." *Christianity Today*, November 2007, 80.

17. Ibid.

18. Psalm 19:1.

19. Nancy R. Pearcey, *Total Truth* (Wheaton, IL: Crossway Books, 2004), 188.

## Chapter 4: If You're So Good, Why Do You Allow Innocents to Suffer?

1. Sir Arthur Conan Doyle, *The Adventures of the Cardboard Box* (Whitefish, MT: Kessinger, 2004), 22.

2. Peter Kreeft and Ronald K. Tacelli, *Handbook of Christian Apologetics* (Downers Grove, IL: InterVarsity Press, 1994), 122.

3. Cited in Lee Strobel, *The Case for Faith* (Grand Rapids, MI: Zondervan, 2000), 29.

4. John R.W. Stott, *The Cross of Christ* (Downers Grove, IL: InterVarsity Press, 1986), 311.

5. David Hume, *Dialogues Concerning National Religion* (London: William Blackwood, 1907), 134, 140. Emphasis added.

6. 1 John 4:10.

7. Luke 1:37.

8. Romans 8:28.

9. Psalm 73:3-5,12 ESV.

10. Psalm 73:13-14 ESV.

11. Job 1:1.

12. Job 1:8.

13. Job 1:3.

14. Job 1:13-19; 2:1-8.

15. Job 1:6-12.

16. Job 38:4-5.

17. Randy Alcorn, *If God Is Good* (Colorado Springs, CO: Multnomah Books), 41. Much of this chapter will draw from Alcorn's work, and I am deeply indebted to one of my favorite authors for his valuable insight.

18. Ibid.

19. Isaiah 55:8-9.

20. Alcorn goes on to give several reasons why God has chosen not to make His purposes for evil and suffering clearer. Among these are our finite and fallen understanding, explanations are not always completely helpful or comforting, God expects us to trust Him apart from detailed explanations, and God has revealed enough of Himself to give us more than enough reason to trust Him. See Alcorn, *If God Is Good*, 347-51.

21. Ibid., 350. Alcorn goes on to say, "We share this in common with Job—*God*

*doesn't specifically explain why he permits evil and suffering to fall upon us.* He wants us to trust him. In one sense, Job is everyman" (Ibid., 192).

22. Mark 10:17-18. Jesus was not saying that He Himself was not good. He was saying that He (Jesus) was God. This young man, who prided himself on his goodness and would have been known as a good person by all who knew him, was going to be forced to realize that all human goodness is tainted by universal sinfulness.

23. Alcorn, *If God Is Good*, 112.

24. See Alcorn's brilliant riposte where he argues that the "skeptic tries to hold God accountable to moral standards that can exist *only if there is a God*...If God does not exist, then there can be no ultimate right or wrong...but when he argues against God on the basis of the problem of evil, then he emphatically affirms there *is* such a thing as evil" (Ibid., 113, emphasis added). So whether evil exists or not, the skeptic case collapses.

25. Richard Taylor, *Ethics, Faith and Reason* (Englewood Cliffs, NJ: Prentice Hall, 1985), 90.

26. Alcorn expands on this thought. See Alcorn, *If God Is Good*, 355 ff.

27. Genesis 39:2,21.

28. Genesis 45:5-8.

29. Alcorn, *If God Is Good*, 228.

30. Genesis 50:20 ESV.

31. Alcorn, *If God Is Good*, 228.

32. Bart D. Ehrman, *God's Problem: How the Bible Fails to Answer Our Most Important Question—Why We Suffer* (New York: HarperOne, 2008), 128.

33. Isaiah 53:3.

34. Alcorn, *If God Is Good*, 209.

35. Ibid., 213.

36. Ibid.

37. It was awarded the 1968 Hugo Award for Best Dramatic Presentation.

38. http://en.wikipedia.org/wiki/The_City_on_the_Edge_of_Forever.

39. God either causes or allows all trouble and suffering, and we can rest assured it is all in His ultimate sovereign plan.

40. www.yourlifecommunity.com/?p=669.

41. Job 2:10.

42. Proverbs 24:10.

43. I do not believe in faith *healers*. All healing ultimately comes from God, and normally He heals through doctors and medicine, but He is certainly not limited by these.

44. Job 23:10.

45. http://science.howstuffworks.com/gold5.htm.

46. Romans 8:18.

47. 2 Corinthians 4:17.

## Chapter 5: Is Israel Still Special to You Today?

1. Ezekiel 5:5. The original nations of the earth did not unilaterally choose the lands they would inhabit. Those locations were determined by God's sovereign choice. "When the Most High gave the nations their inheritance, when he divided all mankind, he set up boundaries for the peoples according to the number of the sons of Israel. For the LORD's portion is his people, Jacob his allotted inheritance" (Deuteronomy 32:8-9).

2. Psalm 122:6.

3. Isaiah 19:23-25.

4. http://bpnews.net/printcolumn.asp?ID=2113.

5. Every American secretary of state should keep this in mind as they try to negotiate a lasting peace in the Middle East. It is a difficult, if not impossible, task.

6. Genesis 18:10-14.

7. Genesis 12:1-3.

8. Romans 4:19-21.

9. Israel is so tiny it would fit into almost any state in the U.S.

10. Deuteronomy 28:15,25,37,63-64.

11. There are far too many passages to discuss them all here. I include just a couple in the text.

12. Jeremiah 31:10. The entire chapter deals with the "glorious hope of a restored nation of Israel." R.K. Harrison, *Jeremiah and Lamentations*, Tyndale Old Testament Commentaries (Downers Grove, IL: InterVarsity Press, 1973), 135.

13. Ezekiel 11:17; 36:8-11.

14. http://blogs.usatoday.com/oped/2007/04post_47.html. If Twain understood and believed God's Word, he could have answered his own question.

15. www.mfa.gov.il/MFA/Peace%20Process/Guide%20to%20the%20 Peace%20Process/Declaration%20of%20Establishment%20of%20 State%20of%20Israel. The new state was recognized that night by the United States.

16. www.zionism-israel.com/dic/War_of_Independence.htm. This among many other sites gives a glimpse of the overwhelming odds facing Israel in her first war of independence.

17. In the 1973 Yom Kippur War, the Arabs decided to try again. Combined, Egypt and Syria fielded 1,000,000 men, 4500 tanks, and 1000 planes. Though Israel was caught off guard as she celebrated one of her most sacred religious holidays, within three days her armed forces were within striking distance of both Damascus and Cairo.

18. Amos 9:14-15.

19. Which is why on most of the tours I have hosted in Israel, we try never to be in Jerusalem on the Sabbath. The inconvenience to touring is just too great.

20. Portions of Ezra and Daniel and one verse in Jeremiah were written in Aramaic.

21. See the recounting of this at www.jewishvirtuallibrary.org/jsource/biography /ben_yehuda.html.

22. www.heebz.com/categories.

23. Genesis 12:3.

24. Mitchell G. Bard, *Will Israel Survive?* (New York: Palgrave Macmillan, 2007), 231-32.

25. Jeremiah 31:35-36.

26. Isaiah prophesied that Israel would return to their land like "doves to their nests" (Isaiah 60:8; see also vv. 9-10). A dove has a homing instinct that brings it back to its nesting place from anywhere in the world. Like a magnet, the very land of Israel has drawn her rightful occupants back to her soil. In fact, the Hebrew term for traveling to Jerusalem and the Promised Land is *aliyah*—"ascent." The word is also used to refer to a spiritual uplifting. For a Zionist, a Jew moving to Israel is the highest form of true identification as a Jew, while one who leaves Israel is inevitably committing the sin of *yeridah* or "descent." See Anton La Guardia, *War Without End* (New York: Thomas Dunne Books, 2001), 16.

27. Bryant Wright, *Seeds of Turmoil* (Nashville, TN: Thomas Nelson Publishers, 2010), 169. We must keep in mind that God chose Israel solely because of His

sovereign grace and love, not because there was anything special about Israel herself. See Deuteronomy 7:7-9.

28. D. James Kennedy, *Character and Destiny* (Grand Rapids, MI: Zondervan, 1994), 54. Michael Medved adds, "For most American Jews, the only belief they hold in common is that Jesus was not the Messiah. That's the one thing that defines you as a Jew" (cited in Bob Jones, "Deuteronomy Duo," *World*, February 15, 1997).

29. Jeremiah 31:31-34.

30. Romans 11:26.

31. Zechariah 12:3.

32. Zechariah 14:2-3.

33. Zechariah 12:10.

34. 2 Samuel 7:22-24 (emphasis added).

35. 2 Timothy 2:13.

**Chapter 6: I Thought You Were Loving...Will You Really Send People to Hell?**

1. www.pwc-sii.com/CourtDocs/Transcripts/RochaSharon-VIS.htm.

2. K. Connie Kang, "Next Stop, the Pearly Gates...or Hell," *Los Angeles Times*, October 24, 2003.

3. Mark Driscoll and Gerry Breshears, *Vintage Jesus* (Wheaton, IL: Crossway Books, 2007), 222-23.

4. Song "Imagine" on album *Imagine* produced by John Lennon, Yoko Ono, and Phil Specter, EMI Records, 1971.

5. William R. Mattox Jr., "Hell Deserves as Much Respect as Heaven," *USA Today*, October 29, 1998, 15a. He goes on to observe another curiosity, "Why is it that many of the people who tell others 'to go to Hell' turn around and tell pollsters they don't really believe Hell exists?"

6. Cited by Larry Dixon, *The Other Side of the Good News* (Scotland, UK: Christian Focus Publications, 2003), 42.

7. http://koti.mbnet.fi/amoira/religionsermons3.htm.

8. Matthew 5:22,28-30 NASB.

9. Bertrand Russell, *Why I Am Not a Christian* (New York: Simon and Schuster, 1957), 17.

10. Clark Pinnock, "The Destruction of the Family Impenitent," *Criswell Theological Review* 4, (1990): 246-47. I added the emphasis to show how flippantly

Pinnock takes both the seriousness of sin and the holiness of God. Both need to be understood in order to contextualize hell in Scripture. As Randy Alcorn puts it, "If we regard Hell as a divine overreaction to sin...we deny the extent of God's holiness and the extent of our evil. We deny the extreme seriousness of sin...and worst of all we deny the extreme magnificence of God's grace in Christ's blood" (Randy Alcorn, *If God Is Good* [Colorado Springs, CO: Multnomah Books, 2009], 315).

11. John Blanchard, *Whatever Happened to Hell?* (Durham, England: Evangelical Press, 1993), 128-29.

12. Matthew 13:41-42 ESV.

13. Revelation 20:10 NASB.

14. There is a movement by some to deny any concept of eternal torment as "cruel and unusual punishment." The proposed alternative is annihilation—a complete cessation of existence. The late Clark Pinnock defiantly states, "It's time for evangelicals to come out and say that the biblical and morally appropriate doctrine of Hell is annihilation, not everlasting torment" (Clark Pinnock and Delwin Brown, *Theological Crossfire* [Grand Rapids, MI: Zondervan, 1990], 226). However, Pinnock candidly admits the source of his opposition: "I was led to question the traditional belief in everlasting conscious torment because of moral and broader theological considerations, *not first of all on scriptural grounds*" (Ibid., emphasis added). Pinnock concedes that his primary appeal is not to the plain teaching of Scripture.

Similarly, the esteemed John Stott registers his opposition in these terms: "Emotionally, I find the concept intolerable and do not understand how people can live with it without either cauterizing their feelings or cracking under the strain" (David L. Edwards and John R.W. Stott, *Essentials* [Downers Grove, IL: InterVarsity Press, 1988], 314). Again the primary appeal is to something other than the plain teaching of Scripture.

I am bound by the plain words of Jesus and other Scripture to hold to hell as a place of eternal torment.

15. Matthew 25:30 ESV.

16. Matthew 25:46 ESV.

17. Ezekiel 33:11 NLT.

18. 2 Peter 3:9.

19. Hank Hanegraaff, *Resurrection* (Nashville, TN: Word Publishing, 2000), 79.

20. Paul Copan, *That's Just Your Interpretation* (Grand Rapids, MI: Baker Books,

2001), 103. "The punishment fits the crime because the punishment is the crime. Saying no to God means no God" (Peter Kreeft and Ron Tacelli, *Handbook of Christian Apologetics* [Downers Grove, IL: InterVarsity Press, 1994], 300).

21. Dinesh D'Souza, *What's So Great About Christianity* (Washington, DC: Regnery Publishing, 2007), 290. "In a sense, the gates of hell are locked from the inside."

22. Cited in Mattox, "Hell Deserves as Much Respect as Heaven."

23. Norman Geisler and Ron Rhodes, *Conviction Without Compromise* (Eugene, OR: Harvest House Publishers, 2008), 244-45.

24. Hebrews 10:29 NLT.

25. www.realclearpolitics.com/printpage/?url=http://www.realclearpolitics.com/news/ap/us_news/2008/Apr/01/ted_turner_comments_on_religion.html.

26. Cited in Max Lucado, *When Christ Comes* (Nashville, TN: W Publishing Group, 1999), 123.

27. Matthew 25:41.

28. Timothy Keller, cited by Jeffrey L. Sheler, "Hell Hath No Fury," *U.S. News and World Report*, January 31, 2000, 49-50.

29. Ecclesiastes 7:20.

30. Peter Kreeft, *Yes or No: Straight Answers to Tough Questions About Christianity* (San Francisco: Ignatius Press, 1991), 133-34.

31. Billy Graham, *Just As I Am* (San Francisco: HarperCollins, 1997), 331-32.

## Chapter 7: If You Love Gay People, Why Should I Care About Homosexuality?

1. The editorial board of the *New York Times* declared the verdict "an instant landmark in American legal history" (www.ctlibrary.com/print.html?id=88764).

2. Ironically, Walker was appointed to the bench in 1987 by Ronald Reagan, but his nomination stalled in the Senate Judiciary Committee because of controversy over his representation of the United States Olympic Committee in a lawsuit that prohibited the use of the title "Gay Olympics." His nomination was opposed because of his "insensitivity" to gays and the poor ("Gay Judge Has Proven Record of Impartiality," *San Francisco Chronicle*, February 9, 2010).

3. www.ctlibrary.com/print.html?id=88764.

4. Ibid.

5. Ibid.

6. Walker basically asserts that religious/theological objections to homosexuality and same-sex marriage are both harmful to homosexuals and irrational.

7. Personal email, emphasis added.

8. "The Sex Life of America's Christians," *Leadership,* Summer 1995, 31.

9. Steve Farrar, *Finishing Strong* (Sisters, OR: Multnomah Publishers, 1995), 62-63.

10. I hesitate to use this analogy for I hold in no fashion that the two are morally equal, nor is the former just the continuation of the latter. Racism and prejudice are held universally as morally wrong and condemned in Scripture (see James 2:1-12), while homosexuality is (as will be shown) unequivocally condemned in Scripture and still held by many on various grounds to be immoral and wrong.

11. See Robert Gagnon's magisterial work, *The Bible and Homosexual Practice* (Nashville, TN: Abingdon Press, 2001), 26-30 for a discussion of these accusations and a reply to each.

12. 1 Corinthians 6:18.

13. "The clearest clue that God gives for appropriate expressions of sexuality, the anatomical and procreative complementarity of male and female, suggests that something greater is at stake than even sexual fidelity and physical health" (Gagnon, *Bible and Homosexual Practice,* 466).

14. "The 25 Most Influential Evangelicals in America," *Time,* February 7, 2005 (www.time.com/time/covers/1101050207/photoessay/17.html).

15. "Brian McLaren on the Homosexual Question: Finding a Pastoral Response," Out of Ur blog, *Leadership Journal,* January 23, 2006 (http://blog.christianity today.com/outofur/archives/2006/01/brian_mclaren_o.html).

16. Which reminds me of the wise adage of the great philosopher Yogi Berra, who once said, "A dime ain't worth a nickel anymore."

17. Genesis 2:21-22.

18. Genesis 2:24.

19. Romans 1:26-27.

20. Romans 1:23.

21. Romans 1:24,26,28.

22. "Same-sex eroticism functions as a particularly poignant example of human enslavement to passions and of God's just judgment precisely because it

parallels in the horizontal-ethical dimension a denial of God's reality like that of idolatry in the vertical-divine dimension" (Gagnon, *Bible and Homosexual Practice*, 254).

23. 1 Corinthians 6:9-10, emphasis added.

24. Two of the best are Neil and Briar Whitehead, *My Genes Made Me Do It! A Scientific Look at Sexual Orientation* (LaFayette, LA: Huntington House, 1999) and Stanton Jones and Mark Yarhouse, *Homosexuality: The Use of Scientific Research* (Downers Grove, IL: InterVarsity Press, 2000).

25. Whitehead, *My Genes Made Me Do It!*, 209. As Gagnon puts it, "A theory of genetically determined behavior does not coincide with scientific assessments of the role of genes" (Gagnon, *Bible and Homosexual Practice*, 401).

26. Romans 5:12. Sin is a spiritual disease we are all born with and is inherited from Adam, the person theologians refer to as the federal head of the human race.

27. Romans 1:27.

28. See www.conservapedia.com/Homosexuality_Statistics for an exhaustive list of statistics detailing the health risks of homosexuals.

29. www.lifesitenews.com/ldn/2005/jun/05060606.html.

30. Noted author on marriage and the family David Blankenhorn says that "for almost all humanity, marriage has always and in all places been 'really' about the male-female sexual bond and the children that result from that bond" (Cited by Daniel R. Heimbach, "Why Not Same-Sex Marriage? Gracious Answers to 101 False Arguments." Unpublished manuscript provided to author.).

31. Ibid., 11.

32. Christian Coalition International (Canada, Inc., http://ccicinc.org).

33. 1 Corinthians 6:11.

### Chapter 8: Do You Really Have a Plan for My Life? If So, How Do I Find It?

1. Ephesians 5:15-17.

2. Acts 2:23.

3. 1 Thessalonians 4:3.

4. Proverbs 3:5-6.

5. 1 Timothy 2:3 tells us that "God...wants all people to be saved and to come to a knowledge of the truth."

6. Jeremiah 10:23 NLT.

7. Isaiah 8:19-20.

8. Psalm 119:66.

9. Proverbs 15:22.

10. Proverbs 12:15.

11. Proverbs 15:22; 24:6.

12. 1 Corinthians 2:12.

13. Philippians 4:7.

14. www.flightlight.com/airportlighting/4.0/4.0.html.

15. Pilots often use mnemonics to help them remember the proper configuration. "Red over Red—you're dead" (approach too low); "White over white—fly all night" (approach too high); "Red over white—pilot's delight" (perfect approach).

16. 1 John 2:17.

## Chapter 9: Some of Your Followers Keep Talking About Being "Born Again." What's With That?

1. Not his real name—but pun intended.

2. John 3:1-3, *New World Translation,* emphasis added.

3. John 10:10.

4. R.C. Sproul, *Pleasing God* (Wheaton, IL: Tyndale House Publishers, 1988), 21.

5. John 3:1.

6. Andy Stanley, *The Grace of God* (Nashville, TN: Thomas Nelson Publishers, 2010), 148.

7. John 3:10.

8. John 3:2.

9. John 3:3.

10. "Or *from above*; the Greek is purposely ambiguous and can mean both *again* and *from above*; also verse 7" (footnote in the English Standard Version).

11. John 3:4.

12. John 3:9.

13. John 3:11-12.

14. John 3:7.

15. John 3:13.

16. John 3:16.

17. John 3:15.

18. In addition to the six hundred Mosaic laws found in the Old Testament, the Pharisees added a massive list of other rituals and commandments to observe as well as practices to avoid to ensure complete adherence to the law. For example, no fewer than thirty-nine activities were forbidden on the Sabbath, making it a day of dreadful fear rather than a day of peaceful rest.

19. George W. Bush, *Decision Points* (New York: Crown Publishers, 2010), 31. This is painful for me because Billy Graham is one of my heroes and one of the greatest men of God I have ever met. Perhaps President Bush misquoted Dr. Graham, but if not, Dr. Graham, though perhaps trying to be gracious, overreached here and plainly contradicted the clear words Jesus gave to Nicodemus. More to the point, John Piper points out what a person doesn't have without the new birth. Without the new birth we won't have saving faith, justification, the fruit of love by the Holy Spirit, or eternal joy in fellowship with God; instead we will have unbelief, condemnation, the fruit of death, and eternal misery with the devil and his angels. For scriptural support see John Piper, *Finally Alive* (Fearn, Scotland: Christian Focus Publications, 2009), 60-61.

## Chapter 10: Are People of Other Faiths with You in Heaven or Only Jesus-Followers?

1. www.kingworld.com/release/oprah_winfrey.html. Oprah's show is seen in all 50 states and in 140 countries around the world.

2. www.achievement.org/autodoc/page/win0bio-1.

3. *Forbes,* March 21, 2007, 160. The article goes on to assert that in 2007, there were only ten self-made women billionaires in the world and that Oprah was the richest of the four listed as U.S. billionaires.

4. U.S. Census Bureau, "The Black Population: 2000."

5. www.azstarnet.com/sn/harrypotter/11614.

6. "#1 Oprah Winfrey," *Forbes,* June 11, 2008. She lives on a forty-two-acre estate with ocean and mountain views in Montecito, California, and owns homes in six other states along with property in Maui and Antigua.

7. www.time.com/time/2001/influentials/.

8. John Tamny, "Embrace the Wealth Gap," *American Spectator,* May 8, 2007 (www.spectator.org/dsp_article.asp?art_id=11402).

9. www.time.com/time/specials/2007/article.html.

10. "100 People Who Changed the World," *Life*, August 20, 2010.

11. Steven D. Levitt, "So Much for One Person, One Vote," *Freakonomics* blog, August 6, 2008 (http://freakonomics.blogs.nytimes.com/tag/oprah-winfrey/).

12. www.cnbc.com/id/29961298.

13. www.nytimes.com/2005/09/23/books/23oprah.html?

14. "The Church of O," *Christianity Today*, March 4, 2001.

15. http://en.wikipedia.org/wiki/Oprah_Winfrey.

16. Quoted in *Christianity Today*, April, 1, 2002, 45.

17. Bill Bradley, *Time Present, Time Past* (New York: Vintage Books, 1997), 422-23.

18. *Bible Review* 23/3 (2002): 14-15.

19. Charles Templeton, *Farewell to God* (Toronto: McClelland and Stewart, 1996), 27, emphasis added. Templeton's argument is irrelevant. Numbers have no bearing on truth. If all but one single person on earth believed that the world was flat, that one person would still be right and all the rest of the world's population would still be wrong.

20. Joseph C. Hough Jr., "Ways of Knowing God," *Bible Review* 23/3 (2002): 16, emphasis added.

21. Erwin Lutzer, *Christ Among Other gods* (Chicago: Moody Press, 1994), 20-21.

22. This view at minimum strips Christ of His divinity and relegates Him at best to a great prophet or moral teacher. Those holding this view even disdain the need for "tolerance"—equal truth claims need complete acceptance not benevolent tolerance, according to this view.

23. Dr. Lutzer rightly points out that this view does not in any way conflict with the freedom of religion. Exclusivism demands that all religions be recognized and respected while refusing to compromise the exclusive claims of Christ and the Christian faith.

24. John 14:2-3.

25. www.foxnews.com/story/0293399945.00.html.

26. John 14:5.

27. John 14:6.

28. Bill O'Reilly, *The O'Reilly Factor* (New York: Broadway, 2002), 163.

29. http://forum.sbcforum.com/players-talk/35773-pete-rose-resurfaces-cooperstown.html.

30. Proverbs 14:12 ESV.

31. Ephesians 2:8-9 NLT.

32. John 14:6.

33. Revelation 12:3-9 records a rebellion by Satan in heaven precreation in which a third of the angels followed him to oppose God.

34. Hebrews 9:22.

35. Romans 1:4.

36. Louis Markos, *Apologetics in the 21st Century* (Wheaton, IL: Crossway Books, 2010), 179-80.

37. William Beausay II, *Boys!* (Nashville, TN: Thomas Nelson Publishers, 1994), 23.

38. Kent Crockett, *Making Today Count for Eternity* (Colorado Springs, CO: Multnomah Publishers, 2001), 27-28.

39. Cited in Lee Strobel, *The Case for Faith* (Grand Rapids, MI: Zondervan, 2000), 165-66.

# About the Author

**Dr. James Merritt** is a respected voice on faith and leadership. He is the host of the international television broadcast *Touching Lives* (www.oneplace.com/ministries/touching-lives) and senior pastor of Cross Pointe Church in Duluth, Georgia. Each week, Dr. Merritt's messages can be seen in all 50 states and in 122 countries. He has been featured in several media outlets including *Hannity and Colmes, ABC World News, 60 Minutes,* the *New York Times,* and *Time.*

Dr. Merritt earned a bachelor's degree from Stetson University and a master's and doctor of philosophy degree from the Southern Baptist Theological Seminary. From 2000–2002, Merritt served as the president of the Southern Baptist Convention, the world's largest Protestant denomination, with over 16 million members.

He and his wife, Teresa, are the proud parents of three sons and reside outside of Atlanta, Georgia.

# How to Impact and Influence Others
## 9 Keys to Successful Leadership

A person's character—who he is—determines the impact he has on others. James Merritt, senior pastor of Cross Pointe Church and host of the television program *Touching Lives*, unlocks nine key character qualities that, if consistently exercised and seen by others, will influence them to reach their full potential.

Readers of this book will be motivated to leave a lasting impact in a number of ways, such as

- making sure someone sees, hears, or feels love from them each day
- letting God's joy shine through their life
- being kind to someone every day
- being faithful and dependable
- treating others as more important

No one can do anything about his heritage, but he can do something about his legacy. Beginning today, he can become the kind of person who makes a life-changing difference for others, perhaps even an *eternal* difference. *How to Impact and Influence Others* shows the way to a life of surpassing influence.

To learn more about Harvest House books and
to read sample chapters, log on to our website:

**www.harvesthousepublishers.com**

HARVEST HOUSE PUBLISHERS

EUGENE, OREGON